PROVENANCE

IN HONOR OF ARLENE SCHNITZER

May 12 – September 16, 2012

Jordan Schnitzer Museum of Art, University of Oregon, Eugene

TABLE OF CONTENTS

IN GRATITUDE

Provenance. The word is familiar indeed to museum professionals, collectors, and those who sell to collectors and institutions. It uncovers the history of a work of art or other meaningful object—when it was made, by whom, under what circumstances—and it details its ownership trail. Often, the more illustrious (and proven) its provenance, the more valued the work becomes. And for museums, in particular, transparency and legality of ownership immeasurably inform acquisition decisions.

Were you to look up "provenance" in a Webster's dictionary, the delicacy and complexity of its art historical meaning will not be so apparent. Brevity may seem odd for a dictionary, but under "provenance," you will find two words: origin and source. For this very special exhibition, we can replace those with two others: Arlene Schnitzer.

With the opening of her Fountain Gallery of Art in Portland, Oregon, in 1961, Schnitzer redefined "provenance" for the Pacific Northwest. As discussed eloquently in the following two essays, the first by Lawrence Fong, Curator of American and Regional Art, and the second by Linda Tesner, director, Ronna and Eric Hoffman Gallery of Contemporary Art, Lewis & Clark College, Schnitzer's impact on artists and collectors, both private and public, of this region is unparalleled. Eclectic in her love of varied media, styles, and subject matter, she was—and remains—passionate and loyal to her artists, often personally acquiring work in depth and documenting their developments over decades. *Provenance* also includes the thoughts of artists. And for the catalog, Mel Katz and Lucinda Parker have written about their personal experiences with the Fountain Gallery and Arlene Schnitzer.

There are two ways of thinking when it comes to regional art. There are those prone to dismissing regional artists, relegating them to a lesser art history or talent, which may, or may not, be the case. Then, there are those who favor regional art as insightful expressions of native or transplanted identities. Schnitzer redefines the debate and synthesizes its components. On the one hand, she calls for quality, innovation, even provocation. On the other, she has remained adamant in her refusal to lose her artists to New York City or any other national arts mecca. More than anything, she has persisted in her goal to create a vital sphere of creativity and support for artists in the Northwest, where she can bring national attention to their achievements. Looking over the roster in her stable and the works featured in this exhibition, we find artists known nationally, if not internationally, as well as others recognized as the finest in their region.

And she did more. She nurtured and educated curators and collectors. Museum collections reflect her influence. She and her late husband, Harold, also raised a son, Jordan, who continues the family's collecting passion and generous support of artists and arts institutions.

There could be no better curator for this project than Lawrence Fong, who has devoted himself to studying and championing the artists of the Pacific Northwest, and exhibiting and collecting their work at this museum. His essay takes us from the Fountain Gallery to the present, assuring that its history, and that of Arlene Schnitzer, will forever be honored. Tesner looks inward and focuses on the impact Schnitzer has had on her own appreciation of art, and as such, on her curatorial career.

Every year, the Jordan Schnitzer Museum of Art, which is foremost a teaching institution, provides hands-on, professional learning opportunities to nearly fifty University of Oregon students. Three of those young scholars—graduate students Jeffrey Carlson, Jessica DiTillio, and Anne Taylor—conducted research and wrote thoughtful entries about the artists and artworks featured. Danielle Knapp, David McCosh Fellow Curator, joined Mr. Fong in organizing the exhibition, co-writing the catalog biographies and provenances, and mentoring students. Diane Nelson, our graphics manager, created this beautiful and lasting publication. All of us at the museum extend our deep appreciation to Laurie LaBathe, Schnitzer's executive assistant, curator and registrar, and Barbara Hall, vice president of The Harold and Arlene Schnitzer CARE Foundation, for answering our many questions and facilitating our research and activities in every way possible. This exhibition and the handsome catalog, made possible with generous support from Arlene Schnitzer/The Harold & Arlene Schnitzer CARE Foundation, the William A. Haseltine Museum of Art Endowment Fund, the Oregon Arts Commission and the National Endowment for the Arts, and members of the Jordan Schnitzer Museum of Art, offer but a glimpse into the accomplishments of a true force of nature and culture.

Thank you, Arlene, for giving our region such an illustrious modern history and for loving art and artists.

Jill Hartz, *Executive Director*

PROVENANCE:

IN HONOR OF ARLENE SCHNITZER

The beginnings of this exhibition came from a conversation with Arlene Schnitzer about the contributions of artists to the history of our place and time. Schnitzer's Fountain Gallery of Art, one of the first in the Northwest, provided livelihoods for artists who played a large role in a changing Portland community. Her intuition and early pursuit to learn and understand the arts directly from artists grew into the first successful art gallery in Portland. Today, Schnitzer is as contemporary and trend-setting as she was in 1961 with the founding of The Fountain Gallery of Art. Her first gallery show included works by now familiar artists Kenneth Callahan, Robert Colescott, Carl Morris, Hilda Morris, and Michele Russo, but also pieces by other then-unknown artists, like ceramic sculptor from northern California Robert Arneson. This group of artists—and the hundreds more that Schnitzer would embrace and represent—helped to define, teach, and enrich the visual arts in the West.

In 2007, I met with Schnitzer to learn about the painter Carl Morris. She shared an account of an accident involving Morris and her brother-in-law while fishing in the Columbia River. "He almost got killed in that boat, which happened to be my brother-in-law's boat, and it capsized over the bar. . . . They took turns, [her brother-in-law] and Carl, holding up another friend, not knowing he was dead the whole time. . . . The Coast Guard did another sweep, and there they were. . . . Another twenty minutes, they would have been [all] killed."[1] One anecdote led to another as she shared candid experiences with Carl and his wife, Hilda Morris, and other artists who have become indelible figures in the history of art, particularly in the Pacific Northwest. We agreed to someday continue our conversation. That led to *Provenance*.

Arlene Schnitzer is neither an art critic, nor an historian, yet she has been, and will continue to be, chronicled into the fabric of the history of the region. The artists she nurtured and the collection she founded with the opening of her gallery continue to evolve. However, its significance is just now receiving the acclaim afforded to better-known endeavors by women, such as New York gallerists Edith Gregor Halpert (a model for Schnitzer's gallery) and Marian Willard, and Zoë Dusanne in Seattle. Generations earlier, Portland women played pivotal roles in establishing a culture of forward-thinking in the arts surrounding the establishment of the Portland Art Museum.

As an example consider what happened when American painter Arthur B. Davies (1862–1928) brought modern art to America with his Armory show in 1911. One visitor to that landmark exhibition was Portland art collector Sally Lewis. Two years later, at Lewis's urging, the show's most controversial work, *Nu Descendant un Escalier (Nude Descending a Staircase),* 1912, by Marcel Duchamp, was shown at the Portland Art Museum.

In 1927, Lewis, who became one of the most influential advocates of contemporary art in the West, supported a daring exhibition at the Portland Art Museum of art from the German Expressionist group *Die Blaue Reiter*, including work by Wassily Kandinsky, Paul Klee, and Lyonel Feininger.

While art dealers like Frederic Torrey, who purchased the Duchamp work, Alfred Stieglitz, and collectors like Alfred Barnes, Mable Dodge, Isabella Stewart Gardner and Gertrude and Leo Stein followed closely this sensational development in modern art, few museum directors and curators in the West anticipated or championed the movement. Yet, in Portland, the appointment of Anna B. Crocker as curator at the Portland Art Museum in 1909, the creation of an art school on the museum grounds in 1910, and the naming of modernist Pietro Belluschi as architect for the new facility in 1932, distinguished the city from larger municipal efforts in San Francisco and Seattle.

Regionally, the Federal Art Project, created during the Depression-era 1930s, included an arts center in Spokane, Washington. Painter Mark Tobey returned from Europe because of World War II and joined a faculty that included Seattle artists Kenneth Callahan and Morris Graves, Californian Carl Morris, and his future wife, Hilda Deutsch, from New York. These artists lent credibility to the Pacific Northwest as a region of emerging artistic development in America.

German abstract painter Hans Hoffmann came west from New York to lead the call of art for art's sake, teaching during the summers at the University of California, Berkeley, in 1930–31. Also, beginning in the 1930s, Europeans artists like Anni and Josef Albers, Otto and Gertrude Natzler, and in the 1940s, Marguerite Wildenhain came to the United States, seeking refuge and then influencing the concepts of craft in America. Art museums and schools on the West Coast were engaged in these national trends. Peter Voulkos, a revolutionary ceramicist at UC, Berkeley, would be discussed as an equal to Abstract Expressionists Jackson Pollock and Willem de Kooning. The impact of Hoffmann's Abstract Expressionist painting, along with an equally radical course shown in work by Richard Diebenkorn, Mark Rothko, and Clyfford Still, was felt in the Pacific Northwest. After the war, the Servicemen's Readjustment Act (1944) encouraged G.I.s to enter colleges and universities, and hundreds chose the Museum Art School in Portland. These developments in Berkeley, Oakland, San Francisco, and Portland would later draw the attention of Arlene Schnitzer.

Searching for artists to represent in her nascent gallery, Arlene Schnitzer traveled with her mother, Helen Director, to Mills College, Oakland, California. Carl and Hilda Morris suggested they meet with Antonio Prieto, then head of the Art Department.[2] It was here that Schnitzer first saw a young graduate student, Robert Arneson, creating strange objects from clay. This chance meeting led her to include Arneson's *She-Horse with Daughter*, 1961 (page 24), in the inaugural Fountain Gallery exhibition. Arneson's mythical figure of a strange, decorative horse with human breasts captured Schnitzer's imagination and bold taste in art. "While my mother was talking [to

Prieto], I wandered around this big studio at Mills, and there was a kid in the back making this thing that was just crazy . . . his name was Bob Arneson. He sent me a fabulous piece called *She-Horse and Daughter*. . . . You can see finger prints all over the clay. . . . And I'm the luckiest person in the world to have bought it back. It has such significance to me."[3] Arneson's *funk* sculpture was the first work Schnitzer sold. Virginia Haseltine, who would later help establish the Jordan Schnitzer Museum of Art's Pacific Northwest art and *Morris Graves in Oregon* collections, was the buyer. This first exhibition also included works by Robert Colescott, Sally Haley, Carl Morris, Hilda Morris, and Michele Russo, artists who would have a lifelong patron in Schnitzer.

By the time the Fountain Gallery opened, Colescott was teaching at Portland State University (1957–66); but his loose, gestural paintings of figures and landscapes aligned with his earlier practice at U.C., Berkeley. Schnitzer's deep friendship and support endured Colescott's personal challenges and artistic transformation until his death in 2009. Her account of the first time she met Colescott suggests they were a match from the very start. "I couldn't find his office at Portland State . . . was late, and I was afraid he'd be upset, and raced to find the right room, was totally out of breath, and finally found him and sat down, and there he was. . . . There was something really strong about him, and I couldn't wait to see his paintings, and so he mentioned he was having a show at Bush Barn [Salem, Oregon]. . . . There were some of the most glorious paintings, the big early Colescott with the great big red coffee machine . . . and his homage to [John Singer] Sargent with this wonderful girl with the big bow in her hair . . . and then there was an homage to [Thomas] Gainsborough. . . . That's why the painting I own today, *Sunday Afternoon with Joaquin Murietta* (page 36), which is a satire of an

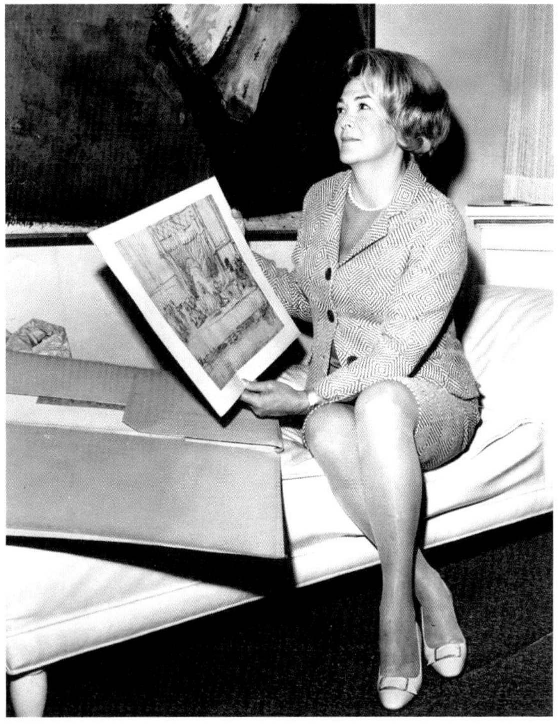

Arlene Schnitzer at the Fountain Galley, circa 1968.

[Edouard] Manet painting, means so much to me, because the very first recollection I had of ever seeing Bob Colescott's paintings were these wonderful, wonderful satires, or homage paintings."[4] Schnitzer was immediately drawn to these expressionistic paintings, with figures enveloped by an expanse of space. "He wasn't a good painter," she said. "He was a great painter. He knew how to manipulate paint to bring out all that exotic emotion of what paint can do to somebody."[5]

The Fountain Gallery's emphasis on regional artists was motivated by Schnitzer's deep commitment to Portland. "I chose to do that gallery in a certain way that reflected me and my mother, who was my partner. [Keeping the focus on regional art] was truly my way of keeping the artists here and living here and being a part of the community."[6]

Another benefit was the opportunity Schnitzer had to learn from artists. In 1958, she began taking art classes but admits at the time she wasn't really *into* art. Manuel Izquierdo, Michele Russo, and others at the Museum Art School shared their respective approaches to art with her. She asked Russo about his compositions. "Do you see that way, or do you just paint that way?" Russo replied, "I see that way. . . . When I'm looking at you, your forehead is a plane, your cheeks are a plane, and your torso is a plane."[7] She also remembers the impact of paintings by C. S. Price, one of the region's earliest modernists. His mural *Huckleberry Pickers*, 1936–37, at Timberline Lodge for the Public Works of Art Project, was on loan to the Portland Art Museum in 1958, when Schnitzer attended classes at the Museum Art School. "I used to see that [painting] on the wall," she recalled, "and I'd think, 'Oh my God, that's so fabulous.'"[8] That response was in contrast to a much earlier response, as reported in *The Oregonian* in 1929. The article "Noted Modernist Artist Adopts Portland as Home" (February 3), offered pointed criticism of a show of Price's paintings of abstract landscapes and figures at Portland's Burlington Gallery in the Meier and Frank Company department store: "My dear, if that's a cow then I'm a horse. . . . What on earth is that, nothing but a lot of color! . . . Give me a nice blue Crater Lake that looks like nature." In Price's art, Schnitzer saw that neither form nor color needed to be true to nature. Price's modernist tendencies would also influence generations of regional painters.

Arlene, with her late husband, Harold, continued to support regional artists and established several curatorial and exhibition programs at the Portland Art Museum. They also have created an extraordinary personal collection of art. In their home, spaces are elegantly designed, from wall fabrics, metallic-leaf cove ceilings, and sophisticated lighting, as a context for an intimate view of the role of art in their lives. One particular space in the living room connects artists from the same and different periods in a thoughtful and provocative way.[9] At one edge, a Lucinda Parker painting possesses the material abstraction that is felt, not just seen. Below it, an early figure and landscape scene painting by C. S. Price shares the painterly movements of Parker's, but not yet its modernist attack with paint. "Look at that Price," directs Schnitzer. "Cindy says how influenced by Price she has been, so how can I not do that? I mean, relationships have always been important to me."[10]

Beach, Low Tide #2, 1954 (page 32) is central to this constellation. The painting was Bunce's entry in the Sao Paulo Biennial in 1955. His cloud-like shapes and vague figurative forms bring to mind Schnitzer's appreciation of the artist's talents. In this particular work, Bunce is not overwhelmed by his earlier encounters with the *Blaue Reiter*, New York's Art Students League, or Jackson Pollock. The painting

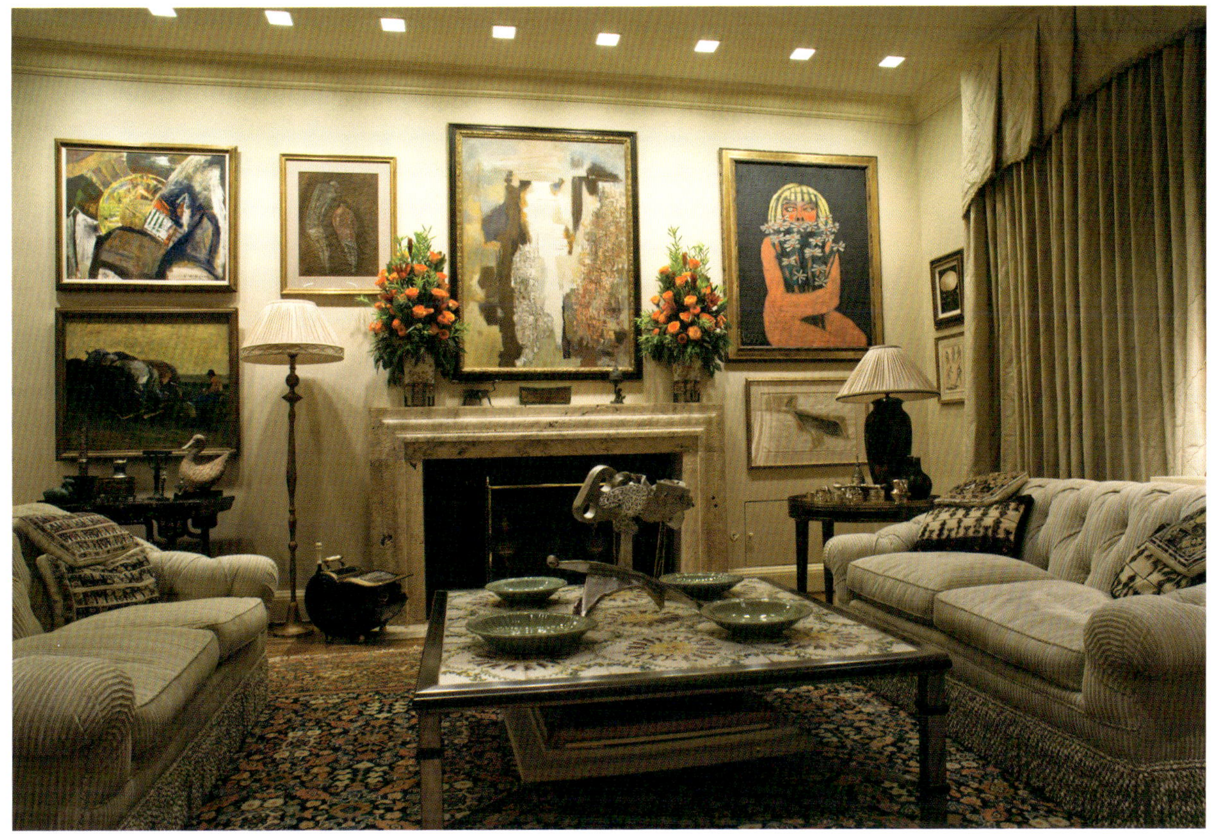

Schnitzer residence, Portland, OR.

emphasizes his attraction to the land, color, and atmosphere of a place in Oregon.

And, on either side of Bunce's art, almost as counterpoints in the conversation, Schnitzer placed Mark Tobey's *Two Market Figures*, ca. 1940 (page 84), and a painting by Morris Graves of the same period, *Bird Having Fed on its Own Heart, Carries the Night*. Tobey's paintings were in early shows at the Fountain Gallery, and his visits to Portland included seeing close friends Carl and Hilda Morris. In this figurative work, Tobey imbedded intricate textures and patterns into the paper. To Schnitzer, it evokes *white writing*, an overlay of brush strokes attributed to Tobey in the mid-1930s. Graves's well-known images are of birds and, later, of flowers. Graves's early drawings of birds came from observations in nature and are simple and ephemeral. In this work and others of the period, birds are wounded, mad, and spirited, symbolizing self-reflection and realization of a world beyond art. Graves and Tobey were acknowledged as key figures in American art with works in national exhibitions throughout the 1940s and 1950s. Here, Bunce's painting is of equal significance.

Striking, in the farthest corner, is Michele Russo's *Girl with Daisies*, ca. 1950 (page 78). The painting was the first work sold by the Fountain Gallery to a business, the Heathman Hotel. It was one of Russo's earliest nudes: set against a charcoal black ground, a young girl with glaring red eyes hugs a bouquet of daisies to her chest. At the hotel it was hung over the bar and, notes Schnitzer, "It caused such controversy. . . . there was some snide comment about how it's obscene. . . . I mean it was just ridiculous."[11] Russo met Schnitzer while she was a student at the Museum

Art School in 1958. He was the first artist Schnitzer approached about showing at her gallery. The name for the gallery was, in fact, his suggestion. Russo reflected, "I think that Arlene had a great many ideals about local artists and was closely associated with local artists, and I think that she showed a great deal of respect for whatever the local artist does. In my own case, I've always felt that I was completely free to pursue my own direction in my work, and I think the work that's shown there in the Fountain Gallery has always had a great deal of diversity and reflects generally all the different directions that local artists happen to be interested in."[12] Disappointed, but never shying from challenges, even controversy, Schnitzer bought back the painting.

In January 1986, Schnitzer closed the Fountain Gallery. About that decision she shared, "I was very careful in selling the really best work to people who were developing a collection. The [Paul] Horiuchi in the hall [*Forms in Red*, 1960] (page 46), was one that I sold to some people . . . who developed a really wonderful collection, which, eventually, they sold off when they moved. My gallery was twenty-five years old. Twenty-five years was the cycle. That was about when . . . their kids were married, they moved out, they were downsizing . . . had to get rid of things. It made me think, well, if I was seeing the work over again, it was time to quit."[13]

One of Schnitzer's most recent acquisitions is Chris Antemann's *An Occasional Craving*, 2011, a finely

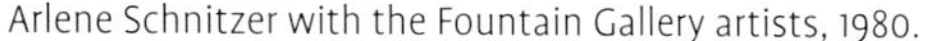
Arlene Schnitzer with the Fountain Gallery artists, 1980.

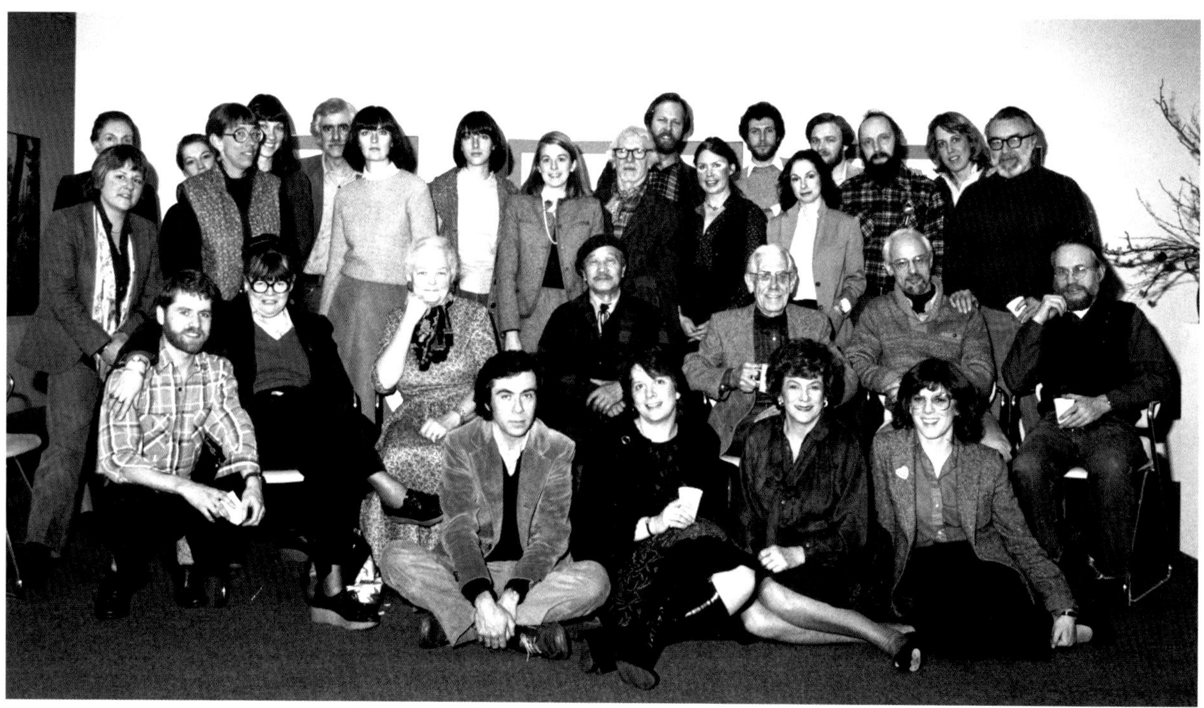

crafted narrative about social class, mores, and gender shaped from clay. With this work, when considering the early pieces by Arneson, one cannot help but realize how far attitudes about art have changed, or not—from *funk* ceramic to refined Meiseian-like porcelain. It wasn't that long ago that the Fountain Gallery was criticized for showing crafts, including ceramics and photography. Schnitzer still hears the pleas, knowing that "artists come and go, and new artists are always there, crying out for attention, needing galleries and an art museum to give them the exposure they need and deserve."[14]

"You do realize, I feel everything I have is on loan to me," she confided. "I don't ever feel that kind of ownership over these pieces. They're loaned to me. It sounds so Pollyanna, but it's the truth: they're going to be here long after I'm gone. Yes, I do feel that's why we're put here, to be stewards. And I know Harold felt that way very strongly. Because I couldn't have done what I did without him."[15]

Lawrence Fong
Curator of American and Regional Art
Jordan Schnitzer Museum of Art

1 Interview with Arlene Schnitzer by Lawrence Fong and Danielle Knapp, Portland, OR., September 15, 2011.

2 Ibid. Upon learning that Jack and Barbara McLarty planned to open the Image Gallery with a few artists Schnitzer had also engaged, Carl and Hilda Morris suggested she visit Antonio Prieto, and also Robert Colescott, who had studied at UC, Berkeley, and was recently hired at Portland State University.

3 Ibid

4 *Oral history interview with Arlene Schnitzer, conducted by Bruce Guenther, June 7–8, 1985. Archives of American Art, Smithsonian Institution.*

5 Interview with Schnitzer, September 15, 2011. Colescott's turn on Edouard Manet's *Luncheon on the Grass (Le Déjeuner sur l'herbe)*, 1863, draws from his hometown lore, Murietta, a mixed-raced bandit-thief, or *Zorro*, set during the California Gold Rush era.

6 Interview with Schnitzer, September 15, 2011.

7 Ibid

8 Ibid

9 December 13, 2011, interior photo by Richard Gehrke, Schnitzer residence, Portland, OR.

10 Interview with Schnitzer, September 15, 2011.

11 Ibid

12 *Oral history interview with Michele Russo, conducted by Jane Van Cleve, August 29, 1983. Northwest Oral History Project, Archives of American Art, Smithsonian Institution.*

13 Interview with Schnitzer, September 15, 2011.

14 Ibid

15 Ibid

ARLENE SCHNITZER, THE INCIDENTAL MENTOR

The first time I heard the name Arlene Schnitzer, the year was 1976, and I was a sophomore ingénue at the University of Oregon, studying art history. I was living in the Gamma Phi Beta sorority, the beautiful Tudor-style manse on Hilyard Street. Arlene's niece, Mardi Schnitzer, my sorority sister and housemate, regaled me with tales of her aunt and her aunt's seminal Fountain Gallery in Portland. I remember the morning, in February 1977, when Mardi, distraught and distressed, reported that the Fountain Gallery had burned to the ground the previous night—the gravity of which I'm sure I was far too naïve to fully comprehend. From this precarious and distant vantage point, I was introduced to Arlene, the glamorous doyenne of Pacific Northwest art. I could not have imagined, at the tender and inexperienced age of nineteen, how much Arlene would influence my own involvement in the visual arts.

No one was more surprised than I at the intensity of passion I found in the history of art. Before long, I had emerged from graduate school in the east and became the director of the Maryhill Museum of Art in the Columbia Gorge. It was there that my nascent tutelage in Pacific Northwest art truly began. It came in the form of exhibition announcements from the new Fountain Gallery. Into my mailbox arrived monthly show cards, beautifully illustrating the work of the most significant artists of the region: Jay Backstrand, Louis Bunce, Michael Dailey, Sally Haley, Manuel Izquierdo, Mel Katz, Alden Mason, Carl and Hilda Morris, Lucinda Parker, Lenny Pitkin, Jack Portland, Michele Russo, and so many more. At the time, I had a bulletin board in my kitchen, and I would post the Fountain Gallery show cards on it, like fancy flashcards that made up my primer on regional art. Regular visits to the gallery helped to refine my knowledge and hone my aesthetic. It is far from hyperbole to say that my education in the history of Pacific Northwest art began in the Fountain Gallery.

Further along in my career, I became the assistant director of the Portland Art Museum where I had the opportunity to witness Arlene and Harold's leadership in the arts community closer at hand. Not surprisingly, Arlene was—and is—instrumental in the growth of the Portland Art Museum. Most indelible to me, however, was Arlene's abiding conviction in what the late Stephen Weil has called "community-centered"[1] museum programming, a compelling argument that a city's art museum must preserve and present the art of the region. When a visitor comes from out of town, what artwork sets the museum apart? What visual experiences make *this* museum unique? Arlene feels strongly that the museum's role is to showcase those artists and work from the community. It is not surprising, then, that the stunning

Pacific Northwest art collection at the Portland Art Museum comprises innumerable works that originated from Arlene and Harold's personal collection or were acquired through their patronage.

Eventually, I left the Portland Art Museum to become the director of the newly established Ronna and Eric Hoffman Gallery of Contemporary Art at Lewis & Clark College. It's a small world: The Hoffman Gallery was designed by architect Thomas Hacker of THA Architecture; Hacker was on the faculty of the University of Oregon's School of Architecture and Allied Arts in the 1970s, the same time I was inhabiting Lawrence Hall as a student. The Hoffman Gallery was designed with two proud plinths flanking the gallery's entrance—twin spaces the architect hoped would feature contemporary sculpture to visually identify the gallery. Harold, a life trustee of Lewis & Clark College, along with Arlene, graciously offered to commission sculptures for this purpose and immediately suggested Montana artist John Buck for the project. As is so typical of Arlene and Harold, they vigorously threw themselves into the process, flying to Bozeman to meet with Buck, to discuss iconographic possibilities for a small liberal arts college and, most of all, to relish time with the artist in his studio. They eventually selected two sculptures from several wood maquettes. Later, Arlene and Harold met Buck at the Walla Walla Foundry to witness the fiery drama of the sculptures being cast, listening carefully as Buck discerned the proper patina. It was apparent that this couple could not have been more engaged had the sculptures been destined for their own home. In the end, Lewis & Clark College received two monumental John Buck sculptures, *Music in the Sky* and *The Hawk and the Dove* (1999). Each of Buck's figures balances a constellation of symbols pertaining to the disciplines of the liberal arts. Not surprisingly, these public works of art have become much-loved and emblematic features on the campus landscape.

While it is impossible to catalog the innumerable ways in which Arlene has embraced, shaped, and influenced the culture of our regional arts community, I am confident that the legacy she takes most pride and pleasure in is the commitment her son, Jordan Schnitzer, has made to the field of contemporary art. Of course, Jordan's youth was inculcated by the love of art. He was not only physically surrounded by the most magnificent examples of contemporary art, he participated in the genuine relationships with the artists whom his mother represented and collected. Jordan continues to support the artists of the Pacific Northwest, but his deepest enthusiasm is for printmaking, for collecting, and documenting the most important works of art on paper by twentieth and twenty-first century artists. Jordan energizes his collection by making it available to the public—to date, more than fifty museums have mounted exhibitions from his collection. Without a doubt, Arlene and Harold's most lasting bequest to our community has been the modeling of a philanthropic dogma that has been passed on to the next generation. Their influence has lasting reverberations for all of us dedicated to the visual arts.

Linda Tesner
Director, Ronna and Eric Hoffman Gallery of Contemporary Art, Lewis & Clark College

1. Stephen E. Weil, "A Meditation on Small and Large Museums," in *Rethinking the Museum and Other Meditations* (Washington, D.C., Smithsonian Institution Press, 1990), 27–41.

THINKING OF ARLENE

AND THE FOUNTAIN GALLERY

I met Arlene in 1964 when I was a visiting artist at the Museum Art School (now, Pacific Northwest College of Art). We had many conversations about art, and after visiting my studio, Arlene invited me to join her Fountain Gallery. I was given my first solo exhibition in 1967, the first of many. As our friendship developed I was impressed with her passion for art and her desire to promote artists' work in a professional manner, a priority of the Fountain Gallery.

At that time, when galleries were new to Portland, she had the foresight to exhibit important artists in the Northwest who ranged from early masters C. S. Price and Mark Tobey to contemporary mainstays—Louis Bunce, Manuel Izquierdo, and Mike Russo. I remember having a show in 1979 that also was part of a show she arranged with a gallery in New York, introducing these heavy-weight artists (including paintings by Sam Frances, Hans Hoffman, Robert Rauschenberg, and Andy Warhol and sculpture by Louise Nevelson) to Portland. That's where I come from, Brooklyn. It was very nice. She also presented emerging artists, who, over the years, have been honored for their challenging work.

The gallery offered innovative events—lectures, talks and poetry reading—and became a community gathering place that gave new audiences a view of the creative issues being considered in the arts. Her ability to promote a climate for cultural diversity—still new to Portland—showed her risk-taking manner, similar to the artists she represented.

In 1972, Mike Russo, Jay Backstrand, and I co-founded the Portland Center for the Visual Arts, a pace-setting contemporary exhibition and performance space that presented national and regional artists, including Trisha Brown, John Cage, Dan Flavin, Phillip Glass, Dexter Gordon, Sol Lewitt, Agnes Martin, Max Roach, Richard Serra, and Frank Stella. From the very start, Arlene was a strong advocate for this auspicious idea. She invested time, energy, and financial support necessary to realize this vision. The PCVA became a ground-breaking organization for alternative spaces in the country and gave Portland a national reputation. I attribute a good part of our success to Arlene's patronage and participation. Over time, Arlene got even better at being exceptional.

After twenty-five years, Arlene closed the Fountain Gallery in 1986. Her long-held view to promote and encourage Northwest artists became a role model for today's galleries and laid the groundwork for the visual arts to be a strong cultural asset in our community. She was ahead of her time.

Finally, she makes the best chopped liver I've had.

Mel Katz

AN APPRECIATION:

ARLENE AND THE FOUNTAIN GALLERY

Arlene never does anything halfway. Fifty (?!) years ago, when she started her gallery in Portland, she put her whole energy, considerable resources, personal charm, and brains into the effort. A gallery exists as a connective valve, or a lens, between the private world of the artist, brooding over his intensely personal studio practice, and the public, people who want to look at art up close and maybe even buy it. To run a successful gallery you must be simultaneously tuned to both artists and viewers (and you have to pick the right artists). Arlene did this over and over in a seemingly effortless continuum of generosity, enthusiasm, and optimism. In her mind's eye, she imagined all those empty walls throughout the city and saw really good original paintings and sculpture finding a home in houses, offices, lobbies, apartment buildings, and public buildings.

Convincing people that art has value always started with herself. She used to buy a work out of every single exhibition that she put up in her gallery. She was not shy about telling family and friends to follow suit (which they did). Every sale of a piece of art helped swell a wave of acquisition that benefited other local artists. Could artists imagine making a living? Arlene reminded us that we could at least think it. Interestingly, Arlene was tenaciously loyal to her artists even during bleak times. The fear of not selling must be courageously ignored by both artist and dealer, while the artist makes the best damn work he can and the dealer leaps through hoops to sell it.

What I remember most strongly is the excitement of new shows each month, hung on gorgeous clean walls with good lighting, feeling that a feast was being laid for all of us, both visual and spiritual. These were shows by artists of authentic integrity producing intensely intentional work: my teachers, Bunce, Russo, Katz, Colescott, all looking awfully good.

At this juncture, I got to know Arlene. I'd come back to Portland in 1969, after getting an MFA at Pratt Institute in Brooklyn. Born and raised in Boston, I had started Reed in '60, then joined the Museum Art School combined program, finishing in '66. So I knew the art scene here just as it was beginning to expand, in no small part because of Arlene. I got down to work in my studio in those early years, getting a body of work together and trying to find a place to show. After many failed attempts, I finally landed an exhibition at Marylhurst (before, the Art Gym). I was lucky to get reviewed, with a photo in *The Oregonian*, written by a very young Roger Hull. A few weeks later, I was at the Fountain Gallery when Arlene said, "What a great review. Why didn't you come to me and ask for a show?" "Well," I said, "I was scared to death of you; this is such a great gallery, I thought I didn't have a chance in the world." Which, of course, she loved. This was the beginning of a long working partnership, which really pushed me to try over and over to make a better painting. I had to measure up to my teachers while their words of exhortation and admonition were still bouncing in my head. I had to measure up to those beautiful walls. Not to mention all my favorite artists from history. Like climbing uphill with wind in your face.

My latest chapter with Arlene was a wonderful fused glass project, 36 x 96 inches, which I built with Ray Ahlgren and Jeff Wallin at Firearts Glass in 2010. The whole process was enthralling, starting with a raft of linear studies trying to find the motif, then enlargements, collages, and mock-up paintings on cardboard. I took these last things to her house to check placements, sight lines, and size. She kept saying, "bigger, bigger." Then, finally, we built it. I spent two months every day at the hot shop, layering sandwiches of plate glass and colored glass paste, slathering, scraping, drizzling, painting. Then, we fired, decided cut lines, and assembled the thing piece by piece on a flat work table. To see it from a distance we climbed onto the shop roof and looked down on it. Finally, we fused it into one large piece, three days heating up in the kiln, three days of cooling off. What we wanted was jazzy glass translucency together with the visual structure of a painting and the illusion of an object. It hangs on the outside grey wall of the house facing north. At night it is lit from above; during the day it collects ambient daylight. The Evening Sun. Arlene never does anything halfway.

Lucinda Parker

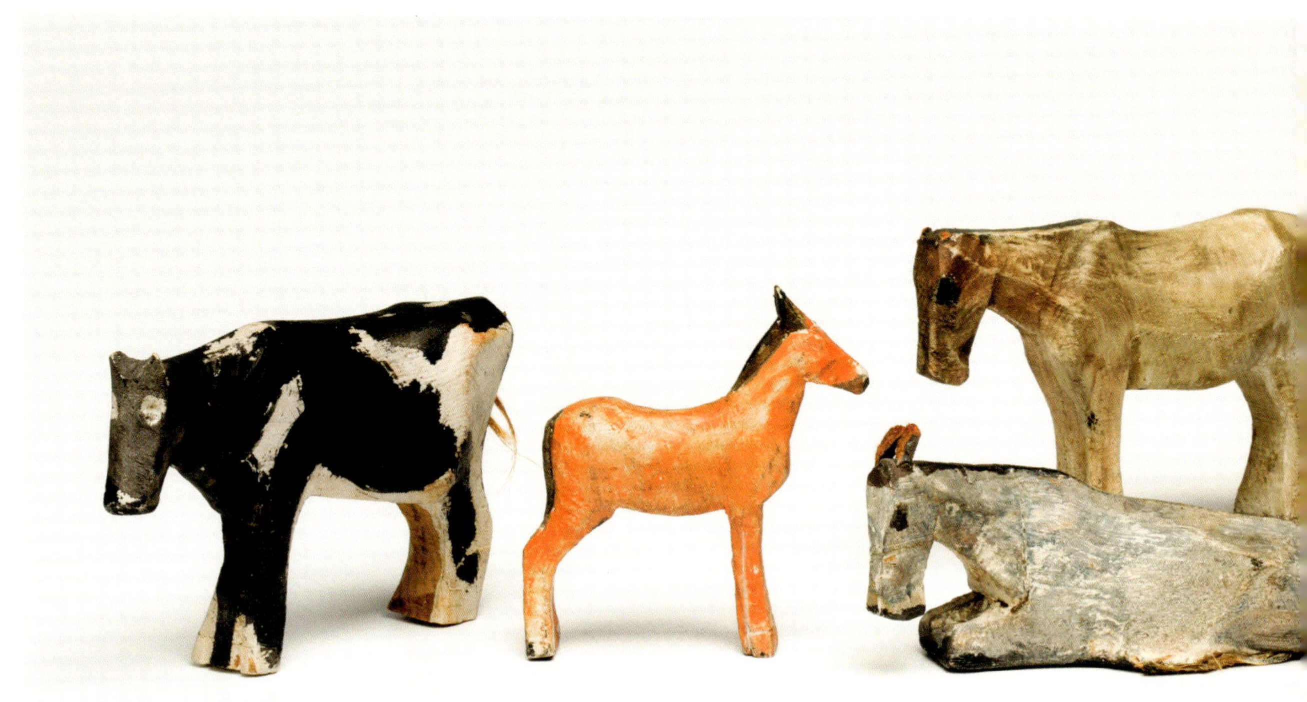

C. S. PRICE

Handcarved animal figures, 1937

Wood, variable dimensions

PROVENANCE

Collection of Mr. and Mrs. James Van Evera Bailey

Collection of Arlene and Harold Schnitzer (November 25, 1971–)

EXHIBITION HISTORY

C.S. Price: Landscape, Image, and Spirit, Jordan Schnitzer Museum of Art, Eugene, OR (October 30, 1998–January 3, 1999)

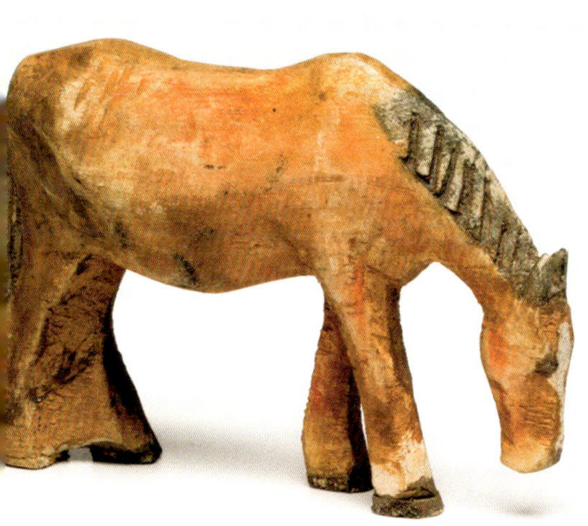

Artists represented in

PROVENANCE

IN HONOR OF ARLENE SCHNITZER

Katherine Ace
Robert Arneson
Jay Backstrand
Rick Bartow
Louis Bunce
Robert Colescott
Roy De Forest
Betty Feves
Morris Graves
Gregory Grenon
Paul Horiuchi
Fay Jones
Jun Kaneko
Mel Katz
Stanislav Libensky and Jaroslava Brychtová
Sherry Markovitz
Carl Morris
William Morris
Deborah Oropallo
Henk Pander
Lucinda Parker
Jack Portland
C. S. Price
René Rickabaugh
Michele Russo
Akio Takamori
Mark Tobey

KATHERINE ACE

(b. 1953, Chicago, IL; currently lives in Portland, OR)

Alleged Songs, 2003

Alkyd/mixed media on canvas, 30 x 30 inches

PROVENANCE

Froelick Gallery, Portland, OR (2003)

Collection of Arlene and Harold Schnitzer (November 6, 2003–)

EXHIBITION HISTORY

Gallery Artists Group Show, Froelick Gallery, Portland, OR (2003)

Katherine Ace received her BA (major in ceramics and minor in painting) from Knox College, Galesburg, IL, in 1975. She moved to Oregon, where she maintains a permanent studio, in 1990, after time spent working as a street artist, corporate portraitist, and graphic designer across the country. Drawing inspiration from several sources, including her deep appreciation for western art traditions as diverse as Dutch still life painting, Surrealism, and Abstract Expressionism, Ace considers her artwork to be a personal method of storytelling. She describes her paintings as having a "feminist orientation"[1] and her process as combining the intentional with the accidental, an effect that can be witnessed in her richly textured application of paint. Public commissions include One Percent for Art projects at the Oregon State University Valley Library (1997) and the Southern Oregon University Center for the Arts (1999).

Ace's *Alleged Songs* showcases the artist's characteristic attention to detail and her delight in unexpected, dreamlike elements. Here, Ace has gathered, both visually and physically, a menagerie of small objects with which she constructed a tree stump. The tactile surface of the trunk is immediately noticeable to the viewer and rivals the exquisitely detailed painted surroundings—which include, among other elements, a folded newspaper and vase of flowers, images that frequently appear in many of her other works—in delicacy and visual impact. Tiny scissors, pins, miniature doll figures, and unrecognizable three-dimensional forms are amalgamated to compose the tree's rough surface, perhaps alluding to the pulling together of the myriad stories and historical references that Ace finds so inspiring. She prefers to leave the meanings open to viewers' interpretations. In the case of *Alleged Songs,* her intentions for making this painting changed as she worked on it; at a certain point, the "painting just took over."[2]

1 "Katherine Ace Biography," http://www.katherineace.com. Accessed February 14, 2012.

2 Quote from the artist. Email from Charles Froelick to Lawrence Fong, February 2, 2012.

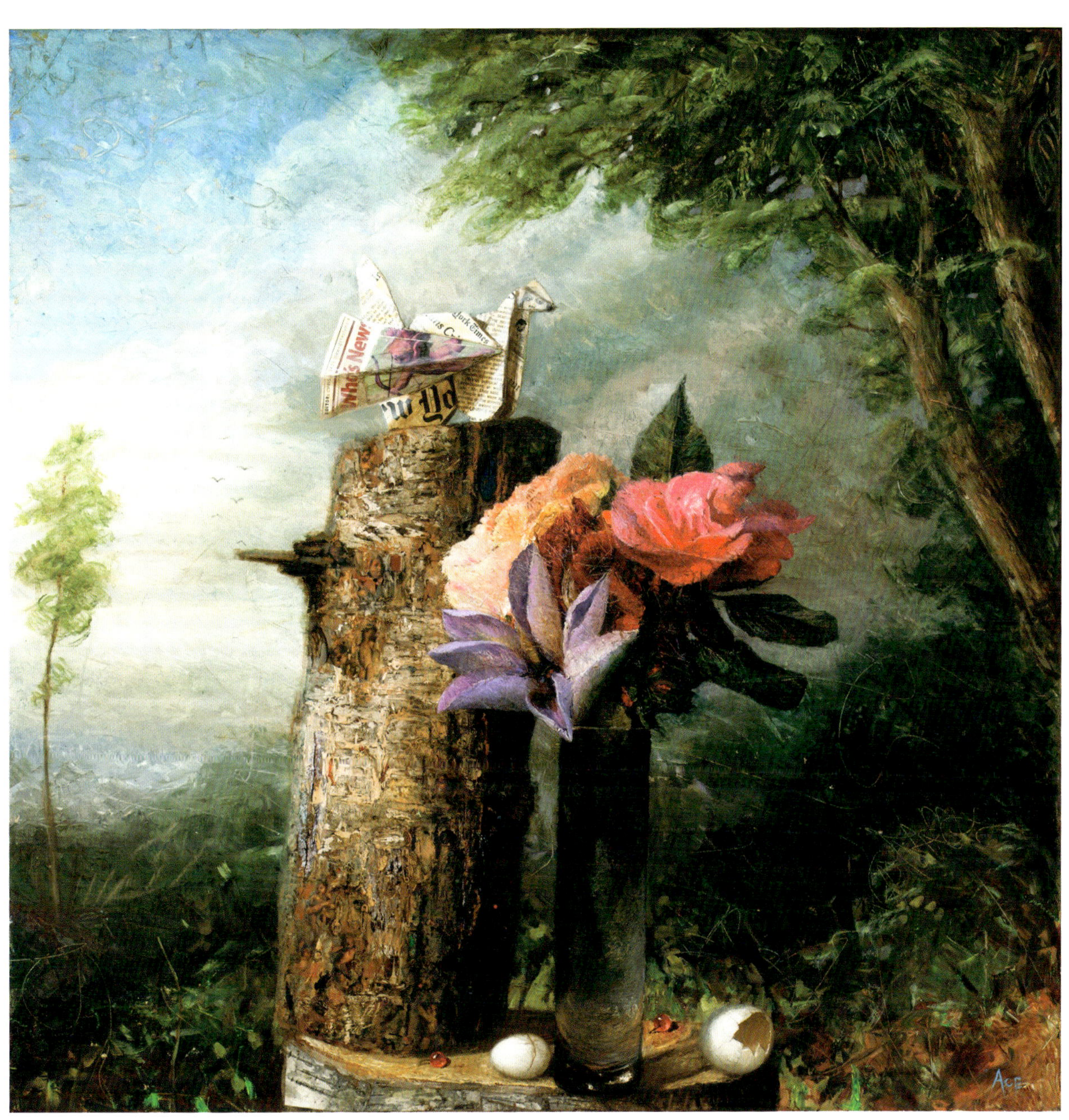
Who's New

ROBERT ARNESON

(b. 1930, Benicia, CA; d. 1992, Benicia, CA)

She-Horse with Daughter**, 1961**

Ceramic, 21 x 8 x 24 inches

PROVENANCE

The Fountain Gallery of Art, Portland, OR (1961)

Collection of Virginia Haseltine (1961–75)

Collection of James Haseltine (1975–2008)

Collection of Arlene and Harold Schnitzer (October 17, 2008–)

EXHIBITION HISTORY

Opening Exhibition, The Fountain Gallery of Art, Portland, OR (November 1961)

Robert Arneson: From the 60's, Brian Gross Fine Art, San Francisco, CA (February 14–March 29, 2008)

Robert Arneson earned his BA in Art Education from California College of the Arts in Oakland (1954) and then received his MFA in Ceramics from Mills College (1958). He became the chair of the Ceramics Department at the University of California, Davis, in 1962 and worked there, despite the difficulties caused by his long battle with cancer, until his retirement in 1991. His presence is still felt on the California campus, where his series of large and whimsical *Egghead* sculptures has been installed since 1991. He received numerous awards for both his studio practice and his teaching, and his work is in national and international public collections, including the Art Institute of Chicago, the Los Angeles County Museum of Art, the Whitney Museum of American Art and the Museum of Modern Art in New York, the San Francisco Museum of Modern Art, and the Stedelijk Museum in Amsterdam. Arneson is often remembered as a key figure in "Funk Art," a movement of California artists who rejected the tradition of functional ceramic art in favor of something more expressive and confrontational.

Schnitzer first met Arneson at Mills College, when he was a teaching assistant in the studio class of Tony Prieto. She was immediately impressed by his work and asked if he would be interested in showing at the new gallery she was opening in Portland. For the first exhibition at the Fountain Gallery, Arneson submitted *She-Horse with Daughter,* a black ceramic sculpture that is a blend of figuration and abstraction, of eroticism and humor. Art historian Peter Selz has described this work as "wildly baroque," emphasizing the sculpture's punning humor (on the word sea horse) and mystical vision.[1] Schnitzer particularly appreciated the sculpture's tactile qualities, saying: "I love it. And you can see his fingerprints all over this clay, and this trunk, with this little, tiny figure. And he sent it to me, and it was the first thing I sold, the day of the opening to Virginia Haseltine. And I'm the luckiest person in the world to have bought it back. It has such significance to me."[2]

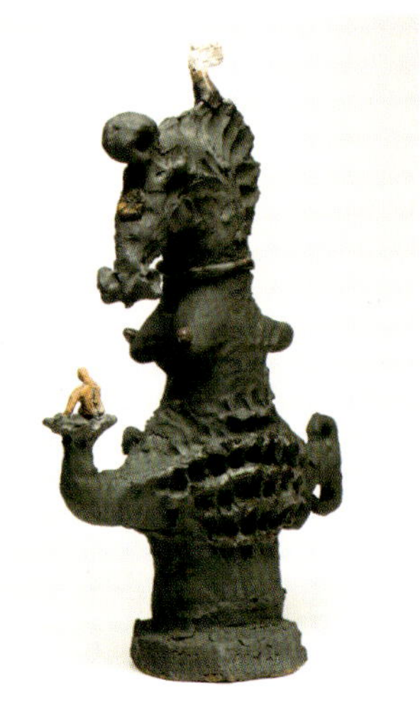

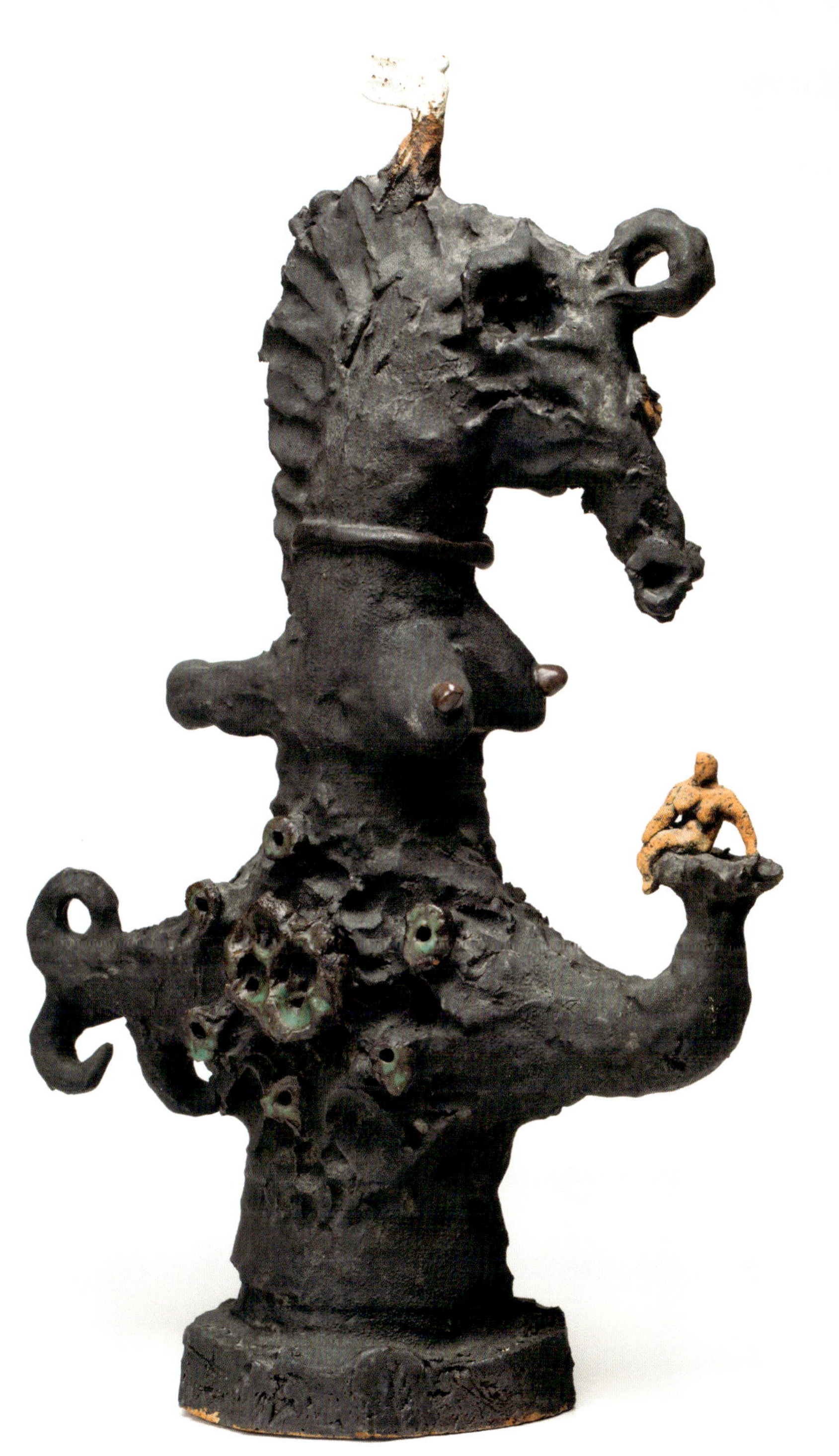

ROBERT ARNESON

Untitled (Torso), n.d.

Ceramic weed pot, 6 ½ x 7 ¼ inches

PROVENANCE

The Fountain Gallery of Art, Portland, OR (1961)

Collection of Arlene and Harold Schnitzer (November 26, 1961–)

Untitled (Torso) is another of Schnitzer's treasured pieces that, like *She-Horse with Daughter,* shows Arneson's expressive capacity with clay. Schnitzer owns several of his early weed pots, a genre of vessels meant for holding a single stem of grass or weed that usually deviated from traditional vase shapes. Arneson transformed this functional object into a squat, headless figure that seems to vacillate between representation and submission to the heavy materiality of the clay. The strategy of transposing functional ceramic forms like vases or dinnerware into irreverent and satirical sculptures was a frequent theme in Arneson's work. Selz attributes this theme partially to the influence of ceramic artist Peter Voulkos, whose tactile Abstract Expressionist sculptures pushed ceramics securely from craft to fine art. Arneson, however, went further to "subvert what had been considered passable as art."[3] For example, in homage to Marcel Duchamp, Arneson produced a large series of toilet sculptures, whose scatological glazes and absurd imagery challenged aesthetic notions about fine art ceramics. While perhaps not as confrontational as the toilets, Arneson's *Untitled (Torso)* rejects conventionally elegant representations of the female form in art in favor of an image that sensuously emphasizes the solidity of its medium.

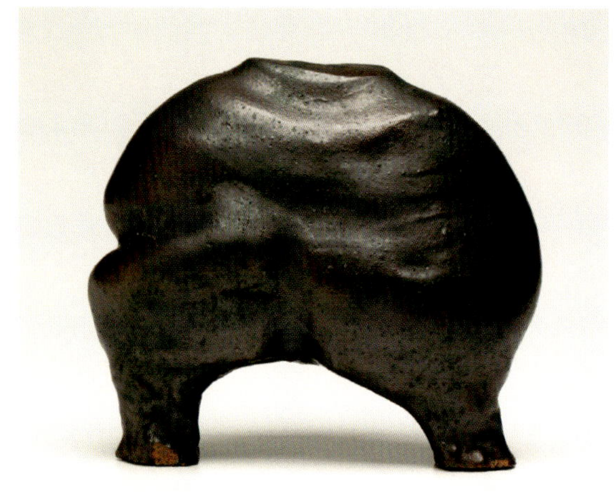

1 Peter Selz, *Robert Arneson from the 60's* (San Francisco, CA: Brian Gross Fine Art, 2008), 2.

2 Interview with Arlene Schnitzer by Lawrence Fong and Danielle Knapp, Portland, OR. September 15, 2011.

3 Peter Selz, *Robert Arneson from the 60's* (San Francisco, CA: Brian Gross Fine Art, 2008), 3–4.

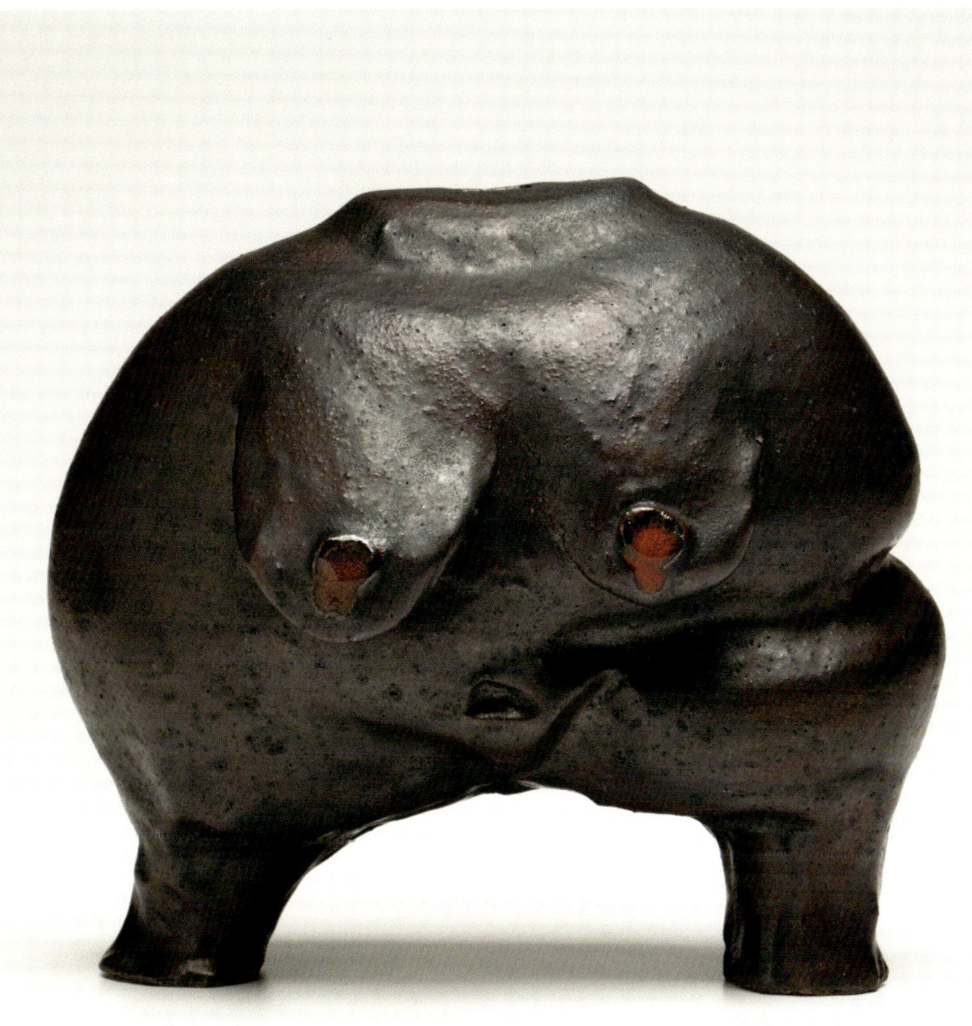

JAY BACKSTRAND

(b. 1934, Salem, OR; currently lives in Portland, OR)

Notes from the Floating World #12, 2006

Oil on canvas, 47 ¼ x 55 ¼ inches

PROVENANCE

Laura Russo Gallery, Portland, OR (2007)

Collection of Arlene and Harold Schnitzer (May 1, 2007–)

EXHIBITION HISTORY

Jay Backstrand—New Paintings, Laura Russo Gallery, Portland, OR (May 3–June 2, 2007)

A product of the Pacific Northwest, Jay Backstrand creates pieces that juxtapose imagery from varied cultures and artistic movements, suggesting congruity between apparently distinct objects and ideas. Best known as a painter, he often sections his compositions in a way that creates a particular space for each element in his disparate imagery.

Backstrand was born in Salem and attended the Museum Art School (since 1980, known as the Pacific Northwest College of Art; Backstrand would later be hired as an instructor there) in Portland from 1958 to 1961. He earned a Fulbright fellowship and continued his education at the Slade School, University of London, from 1964 to 1965. Backstrand, Mel Katz, and Michele Russo cofounded the Portland Center for the Visual Arts in the early 1970s, providing an unprecedented forum for engagement between Northwest artists and artists of national prominence working in New York, Los Angeles, and other major centers of contemporary art (John Baldessari, Chuck Close, David Hockney, Nam June Paik, and Richard Serra were among those who exhibited at the PCVA). Backstrand was the recipient of a National Endowment for the Arts grant and a Smithsonian Institute National Gallery purchase award.

Backstrand's father had been Arlene Schnitzer's pediatrician in Salem. Schnitzer and Backstrand took courses together at the Museum Art School. Later she remarked on her classmate's talent: "He used to sit on the end of the corridor with a mirror, looking at his drawings, which were on the other end of the corridor. . . [the art instructor] used to put the best drawings of the drawing classes up on the wall at art school, and I mean, it was just Jay. Jay's drawings were up there—brilliant, brilliant drawer."[1] Schnitzer defended the artist's penchant for employing imagery from art of different periods and cultures. In *Notes from the Floating World #12,* Eastern and Western traditions commingle, as Backstrand references ancient abstracted statuary, *japonisme*, Picasso, and the decorative patterning of craftwork.

1 Interview with Schnitzer, September 15, 2011.

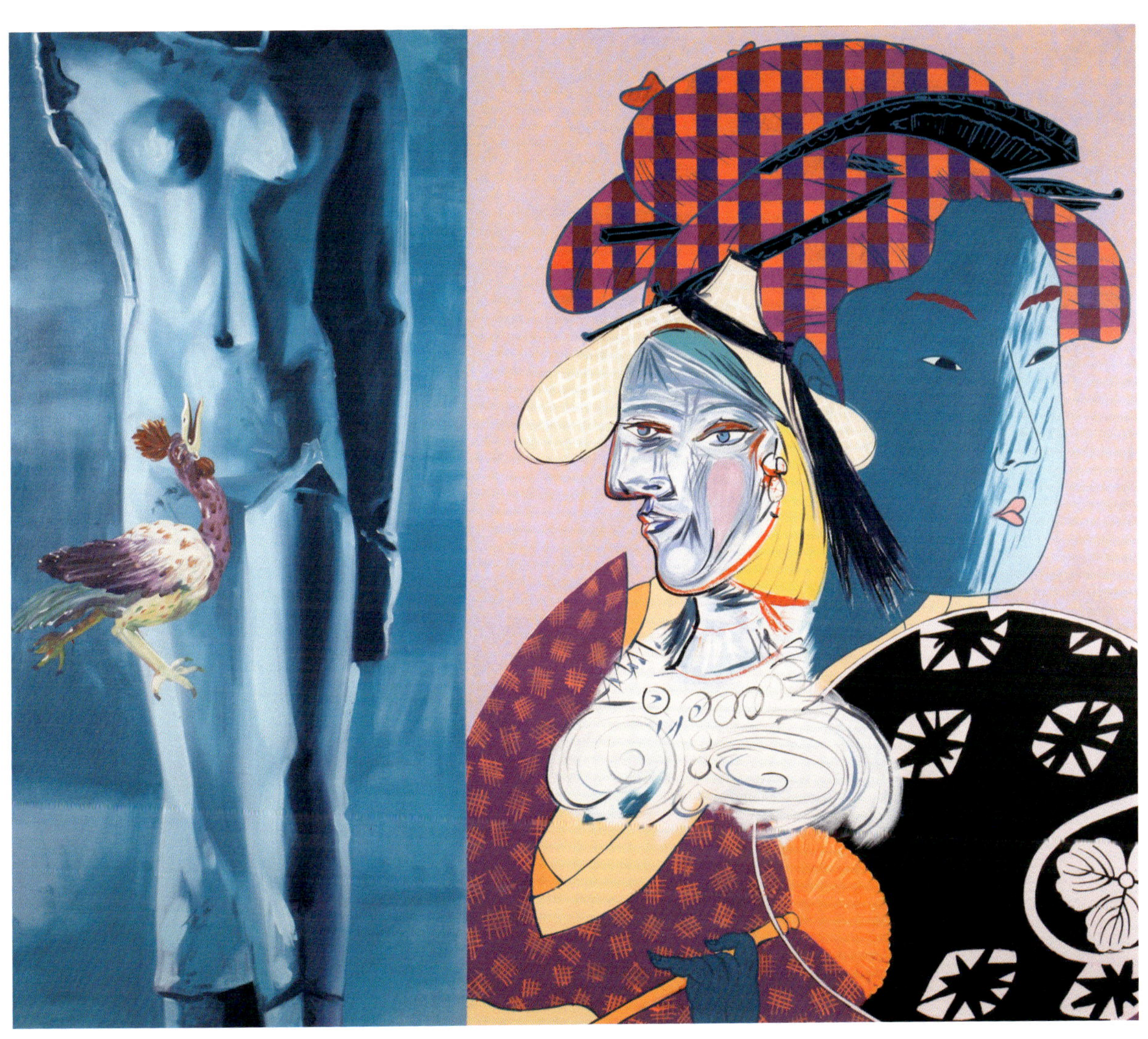

RICK BARTOW

(b. 1946, Newport, OR; currently lives in Newport, OR)

Bear with Humor (aka, For Walt Come a Sunday), 2004

Mixed media wood sculpture, 30 x 17 x 13 inches

PROVENANCE

Froelick Gallery, Portland, OR (2004)

Collection of Arlene and Harold Schnitzer (June 8, 2004–)

EXHIBITION HISTORY

Changing Hands: Art Without Reservation 2, Museum of Arts and Design, New York, NY (September 15, 2005–January 2, 2006). Traveled to Eiteljorg Museum of American Indians and Western Art, Indianapolis, IN; Naples Museum of Art, FL; Philbrook Museum of Art, Tulsa, OK; Anchorage Museum of History and Art, AK; Weisman Art Museum , University of Minnesota, Minneapolis; Tucson Museum of Art, AZ (January 2, 2006–May 11, 2008)

Rick Bartow received a BA in Art Education from Western Oregon State University in 1969. Drawing upon his Native American heritage (though his own background is Yurok Indian, he also became closely acquainted with the local Siletz Indian community), psychological trauma as a Vietnam veteran, personal struggles as a recovering alcoholic, and the cultural experiences of an artist working within the Pacific Northwest community, Bartow has described his art-making as "affordable therapy."[1] His expressive representations of himself, spirit animals, and elements of global myths, informed by such diverse inspirations as Native American storytelling and European, Japanese, Maori, and African art traditions, are evocative and deeply personal. Bartow's process often involves a reworking, again and again, of his materials. In two-dimensional work, these can include acrylic paint, charcoal, graphite, and pastel all in one composition; three-dimensional work is multimedia, pulling together both traditional art materials and found objects. Along with exhibiting frequently in the Northwest, Bartow's work has been shown nationally: in 2003, he was featured in a solo show (*Continuum—12 Artists: Rick Bartow*) at the Smithsonian Institution's National Museum of the American Indian.

Bear with Humor (aka, For Walt Come a Sunday) rewards the viewer who takes advantage of its three-dimensionality. Like much of Bartow's output, biographical elements are woven throughout this transformational image. The bucket, in which Bartow drilled two eyeholes, was originally used by his grandmother for berry picking. He often names works in honor of friends or alludes to inside jokes; the titular "Walt" here is Walt Klamath, a Korean War veteran and elder who led a sweat lodge on the Siletz Reservation that Bartow attended. The artist would help him prepare for the weekly sweat lodge by accompanying his friend into the woods to resupply the log pile, and it was not uncommon for the pair to encounters bears there.[2] Bears are of special interest to Schnitzer.

1 "A Time of Visions," Interview with Rick Bartow by Larry Abbott, http://www.britesites.com/native_artist_interviews/rbartow.htm. Accessed March 13, 2012.

2 Email from Charles Froelick to Lawrence Fong, February 2, 2012.

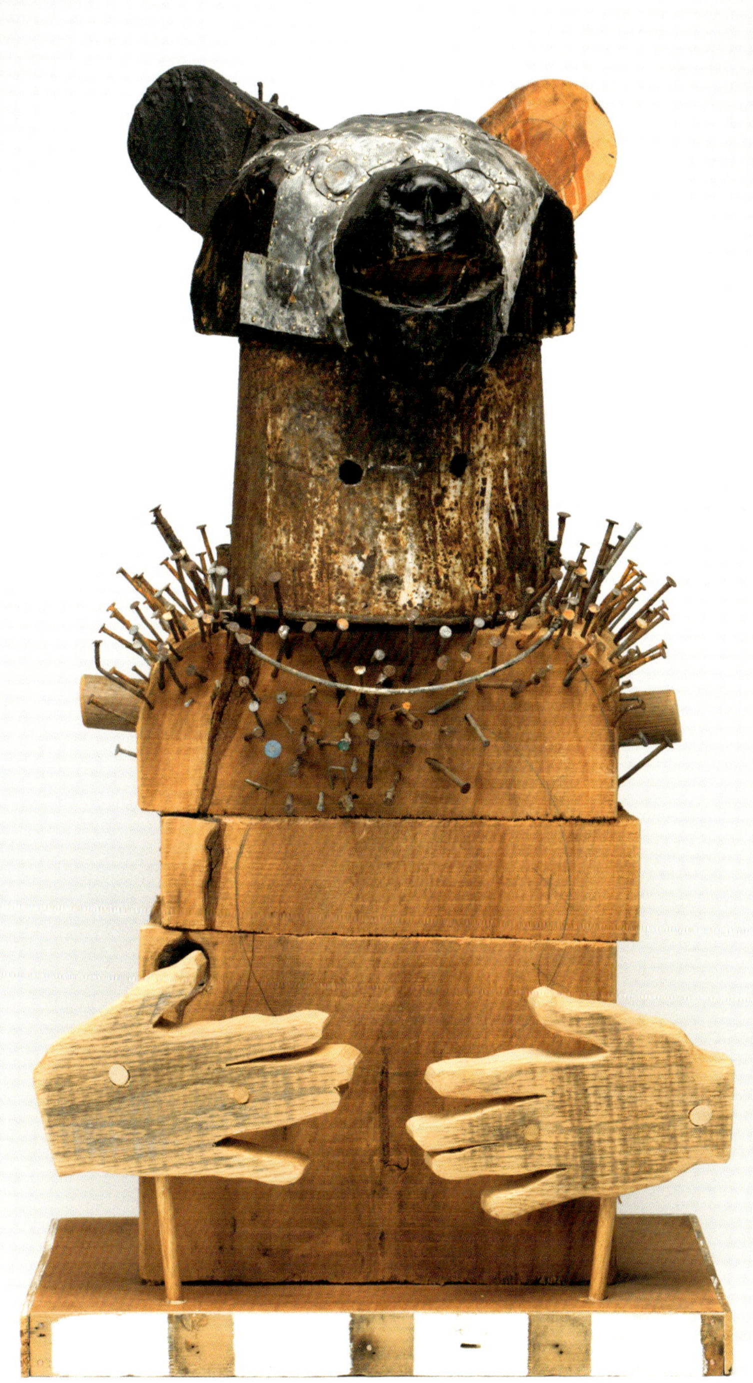

LOUIS BUNCE

(b. 1907, Lander, WY; d. 1983, Portland, OR)

Beach, Low Tide #2, 1954

Oil on canvas, 57 x 42 1/8 inches

PROVENANCE

The Fountain Gallery of Art, Portland, OR

Collection of Arlene and Harold Schnitzer (1974–)

EXHIBITION HISTORY

Pacific Coast Art: United States' Representation, Third Biennial, Sao Paulo, Brazil; traveled to Cincinnati Art Museum, OH; Colorado Spring Fine Arts Center, CO; San Francisco Museum of Art, CA; and Walker Art Center, Minneapolis, MN (1955)

Art of the Pacific Northwest, National Collection of Fine Arts, Smithsonian Institution, Washington, DC; traveled to Seattle Art Museum, WA and Portland Art Museum, OR (1974)

Louis Bunce: A Retrospective, Portland Art Museum, OR (November 21–December 30, 1979)

Portland Center for Visual Arts, OR (1981)

Jet Dreams, Art of the Fifties in the Northwest, Tacoma Art Museum, WA (March 17–June 4, 1995)

PNCA at 100, Portland Art Museum, OR (June 6–September 13, 2009)

Louis Bunce studied at the Museum Art School in Portland (1925–26) and the Art Students League in New York City (1927–31), before being hired under the Works Progress Administration in 1934. Over time, his work evolved from the representational and the figurative to total abstraction. An early interest in his surroundings, whether natural or urban, developed into one of the greatest influences on his own artwork: Bunce effortlessly captured the essence of the landscape in his paintings, serigraph and lithograph prints, and drawings. After taking a teaching position at the Museum Art School in 1946 (where he was an influential instructor for students, including George Johanson and Manuel Izquierdo, until his retirement in 1972), Bunce maintained his ties to New York with regular trips and exhibitions there. He and his wife, Eda, opened the Kharouba Gallery in Portland in 1949 to show the work of the city's avant-garde artists.

Throughout his career, Bunce's unparalleled ability to move fluidly between styles—from Cubism to Surrealism to Abstract Expressionism—invited some criticism from those who thought him too much of a chameleon. For Schnitzer, Bunce represented the best of what regional art could offer. She lamented that "he was always criticized for never sticking to one thing. But that wasn't Louis. And I think he was a really great painter. And I used to say that when all was said and done, you know, in one hundred years from now, [it] will be Louis who sticks out."[1] In the late 1940s and early '50s, Bunce spent most of his summers teaching in the coastal town of Newport, OR, and looking to the seascape for inspiration. *Beach, Low Tide #2* documents the atmospheric, indefinable quality of the Pacific coastline. It is at once both entirely abstract and instinctively recognizable. Schnitzer's appreciation for Bunce's unique talent was reciprocated. In 1982, when asked what he thought accounted for Schnitzer's long-lasting success with the Fountain Gallery, he replied: "Well, I think she was able to support it, for one thing. I think fortunately having the support of her own family, and her husband; this certainly helped. But she had the support of a lot of the artists, too."[2]

1 Interview with Schnitzer, September 15, 2011.

2 *Oral history interview with Louis Bunce, conducted by Rachel Rosenfield, Dec. 3–Dec. 13, 1982, Archives of American Art, Smithsonian Institution.*

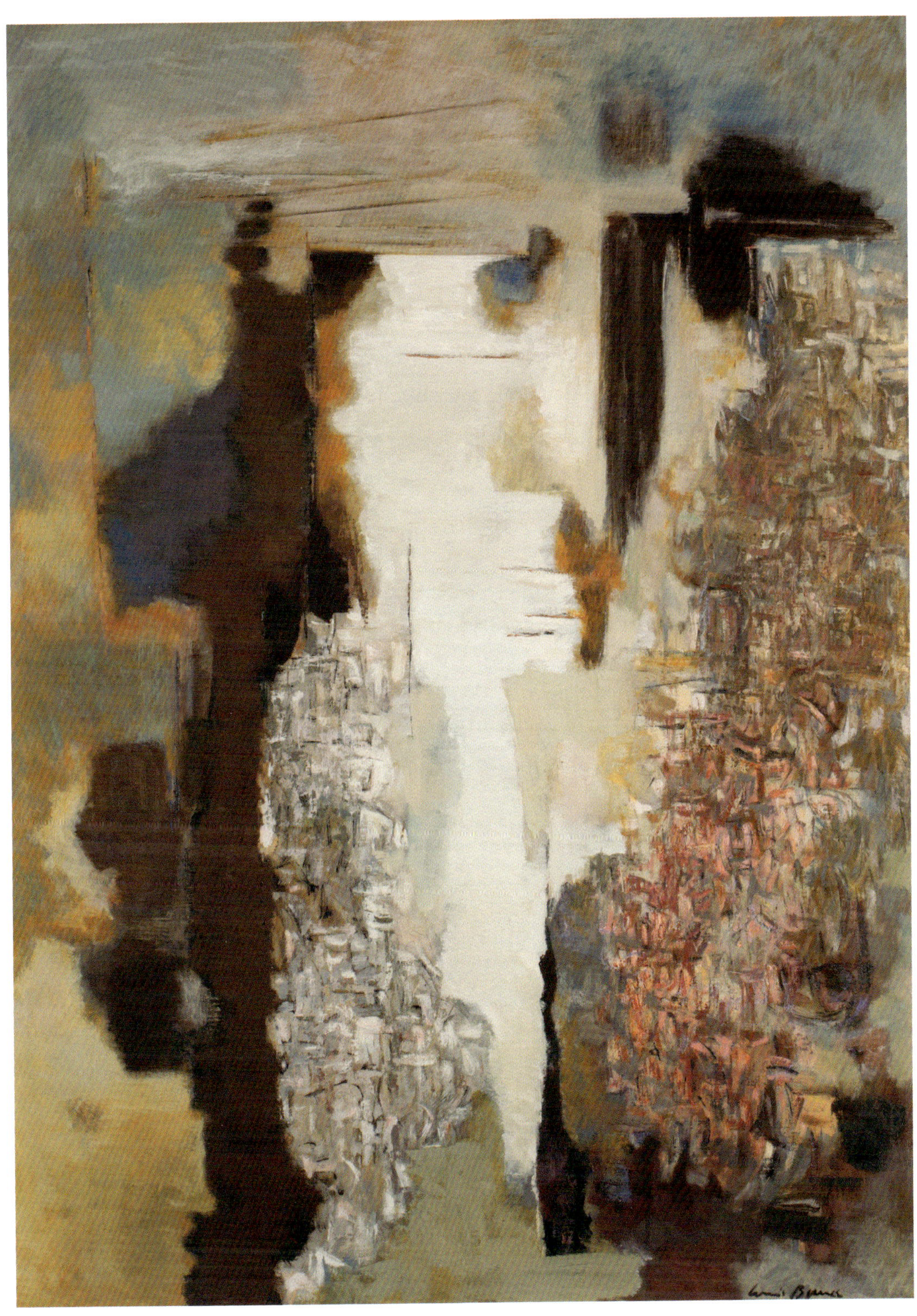

ROBERT COLESCOTT

(b. 1925, Oakland, CA; d. 2009, Tucson, AZ)

I Dreamed I Was Really Good Looking, 1991

Acrylic on paper, 41 x 26 inches

PROVENANCE

Laura Russo Gallery, Portland, OR (1995)

Collection of Arlene and Harold Schnitzer (Jan. 27, 1996–)

EXHIBITION HISTORY

Robert Colescott, Laura Russo Gallery, Portland, OR (1995)

Black History Month Exhibition, Heathman Hotel, Portland, OR (February 1–April 21, 2000)

Robert Colescott received his BA from the University of California, Berkeley, in 1949 and also his MFA in 1952. During a trip to Europe between his degrees (1949–50) he studied in Paris with the French cubist painter Fernand Léger. After his graduation, Colescott taught art in public schools in Seattle and then Portland, where he was an instructor of painting and drawing at Portland State University. In Portland his artistic career was born, with one of his earliest solo shows at the Fountain Gallery. Known for his critical and darkly humorous engagement with issues of race, representation, and social politics, in 1997 Colescott became the first African-American artist to represent the United States in the Venice Biennale. In addition to numerous private collections, Colescott's work can be found in many public collections, including the Hirshhorn Museum and Sculpture Garden, the Metropolitan Museum of Art, the Museum of Modern Art, and the Whitney Museum of American Art.

With its biting perspective on American racial identity, *I Dreamed I Was Really Good Looking* is an excellent example of Colescott's mature style. The thick expressive brushstrokes here serve to depict a dream image that alludes to a Black man's self-loathing in an ethnocentric visual world.

Schnitzer knew Colescott from the beginning of his artistic career, first attending one of his shows in Salem, Oregon, before inviting him to exhibit his work at the Fountain Gallery. While she was already convinced of his talent as a painter, for Schnitzer the critical moment in Colescott's career was his journey to Egypt in 1964.[1] The artist spent 1964–65 and 1966–67 in Cairo, as an artist-in-residence at the American Research Center and then teaching at the American University. According to art historian and curator Lowery Stokes Sims, "The contact he made in those years with Egyptian culture and the African continent sparked within him the realization that his art need no longer be exclusively European in orientation."[2] Schnitzer and her husband, Harold, were in Paris when Colescott and his wife returned there after their time in Egypt, and she witnessed firsthand the profound change in him.[3] Colescott explained, "Living in a culture that is strictly 'non-white'... excited me about some things, some of the ideas about race and culture in our own country; I wanted to say something about it."[4]

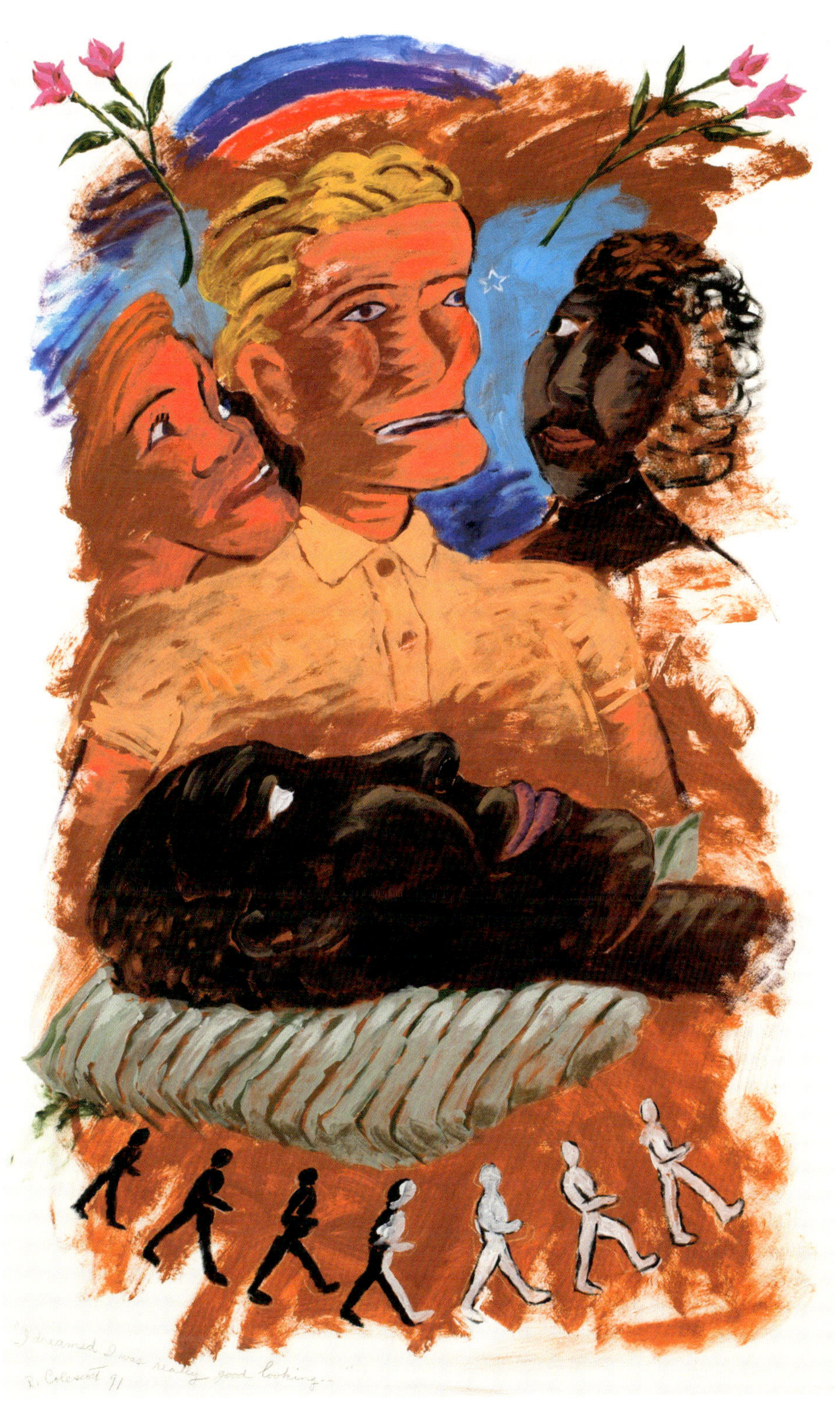
I dreamed I was really good looking..."
R. Colescott 91

ROBERT COLESCOTT

***Sunday Afternoon with Joaquin Murietta*, 1980**

Acrylic on canvas, 72 x 84 inches

PROVENANCE

Semaphore Gallery, New York, NY (1980–81)

Collection of Arlene and Harold Schnitzer (January 12, 1981–)

EXHIBITION HISTORY

Semaphore Gallery, New York, NY (1981)

Not Just for Laughs—The Art of Subversion, The New Museum, New York, NY (November 21 1981–January 21, 1982)

Confrontations (Group Show), Henry Art Gallery, University of Washington, Seattle (August 24–November 20, 1984)

Robert Colescott: Another Judgment, Knight Gallery/Spirit Square Arts Center, Charlotte, NC (February 13–April 7, 1985)

Robert Colescott: A Retrospective, San Jose Museum of Art, CA (March 1987– July 1989)

Purloined Image, Flint Institute of the Arts, MI (March–May 1993)

Sunday Afternoon with Joaquin Murietta is a prime example of Colescott's brand of art-historical homage, which intelligently fuses engagement with the earlier artwork and scathing social critique. In this revision of Manet's famous 1862–63 painting *Dejeuner Sur l'Herbe (Luncheon on the Grass),* the white female is replaced by a subtly smiling black woman clad in nothing but glistening red cowboy boots. This reworking of art history becomes even more complex, with Joaquin Murietta, a controversial but legendary figure from the period of the California Gold Rush, often called the "Robin Hood of El Dorado," and a compatriot replacing the formerly white French men of Manet's original. According to art historian Mitchell Kahan, by juxtaposing this American mythical history with Manet's controversial painting, Colescott "indirectly suggests that art itself is a purveyor of social inequality and does not belong to the realm of sacred truth."[5] Though considered a masterpiece today, Manet's painting was considered obscene and socially inappropriate in the nineteenth century for its frank allusion to sexuality. Colescott has manipulated the work to make it scandalous once again, revealing the art world's implicit, restrictive rules about the representation of non-white subjects.

1 Interview with Schnitzer, September 15, 2011.

2 Lowery Stokes Sim and Mitchell D. Kahan, *Robert Colescott: A Retrospective* (San Jose: San Jose Museum of Art, 1987), 2.

3 Interview with Schnitzer, September 15, 2011.

4 Robert Colescott and Ann Shengold, "Conversation with Robert Colescott," in *Robert Colescott: Another Judgment* (Charlotte, NC: Knight Gallery/Spirit Square Arts Center, 1985), 9.

5 Lowery Stokes Sim and Mitchell D. Kahan, *Robert Colescott: A Retrospective* (San Jose: San Jose Museum of Art, 1987), 26.

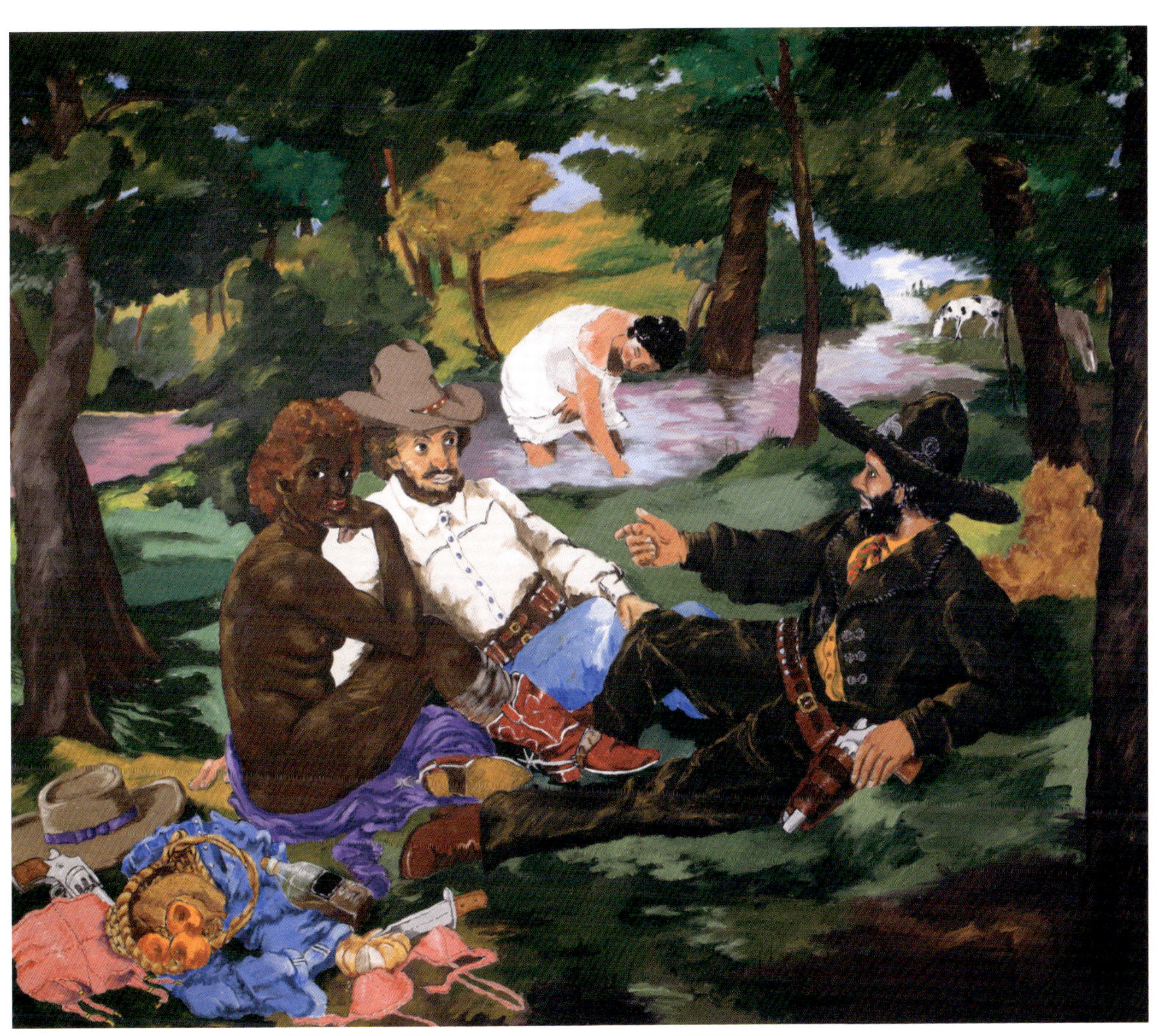

ROY DE FOREST

(b. 1930, North Platte, NE; d. 2007, Vallejo, CA)

All Awash, 1980

Polymer, varnishes, acrylic on canvas, 66 x 72 inches

PROVENANCE

The Fountain Gallery of Art, Portland, OR (1980)

Collection of Arlene and Harold Schnitzer (1980–)

EXHIBITION HISTORY

Three from the Bay Area: Paintings and Drawings by Joan Brown; Paintings and Drawings by Robert Colescott; and Paintings, Drawings, and Prints by Roy De Forest, The Fountain Gallery of Art, Portland, OR (October 10–November 1, 1980)

Contemporary American Art: A Portland Perspective, Portland Art Museum, OR (November 28, 1984–January 20, 1985)

Portland Collects, Portland Art Museum, OR (March 4–May 2, 1993)

A painter, ceramicist, and mixed-media artist, Roy De Forest was devoted to fanciful and chaotic subjects that gave form to his conception of art as magic. De Forest created works with dense patterning that may be read as purely decorative or as sociological and environmental statements.

Born in the Midwest, he was raised and educated in Yakima, WA, in a Depression-era farming family. In the early 1950s De Forest moved to San Francisco to study at the California School of Fine Arts, and from then on he would self-identify with the Bay Area's residents and artistic milieu. He received an MA from San Francisco State College in 1958 and later earned a position as professor of painting and drawing at UC, Davis, where from 1965 to 1982 he raised the program to national prominence, alongside Robert Arneson. De Forest was the recipient of a San Francisco Art Association Award (1954), the Nealie Sullivan Award of the San Francisco Art Institute (1962), a National Endowment for the Arts fellowship (1972) and purchase prizes at the Oakland Art Museum (1956) and La Jolla Art Museum (1965).

All Awash reveals De Forest's proclivity for animalia and vibrant color. The artist crowded his composition with dogs, birds, rabbits, humans, and other ambiguous creatures, all defined by broad, flat planes in bold hues. De Forest punctuated his figures with dots and other abstract designs, so as to eliminate negative space. For all of its dynamic energy, this piece still betrays a definite balance and symmetry. Though De Forest remained in the Bay Area for his entire professional career, his artistic presence extended beyond the region with exhibitions of his work in the Northwest and regular shows organized by the Allan Frumkin Gallery in Chicago and New York. Of *All Awash*, which was exhibited at the Fountain Gallery in 1980, Schnitzer insisted, "It's an important one."[1]

1 Interview with Arlene Schnitzer by Lawrence Fong and Jill Hartz, Portland, OR. November 7, 2011.

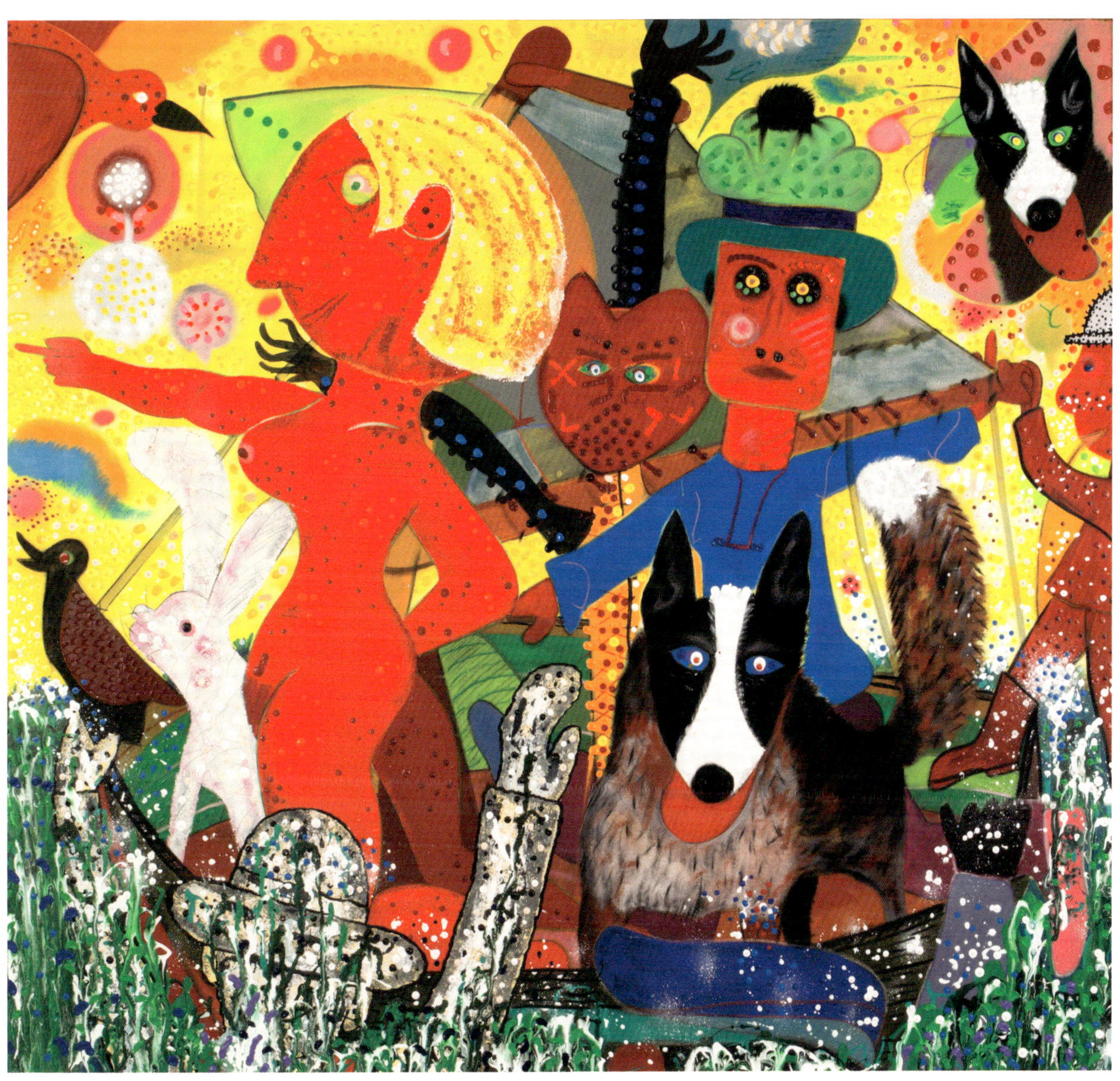

BETTY FEVES

(b. 1918, LaCrosse, WI; d. 1985, Pendleton, OR)

Bonfire Pot, c. 1978

Earthenware, 13 x 13 inches

PROVENANCE

The Fountain Gallery of Art, Portland, OR (1978)

Collection of Arlene and Harold Schnitzer (May 9, 1978–)

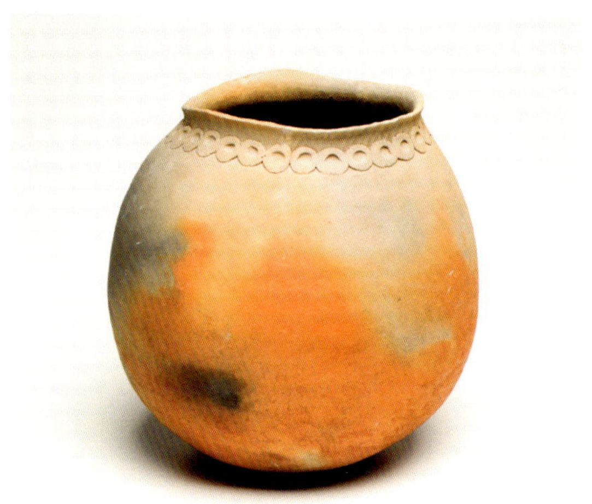

Betty Feves received her BFA from Washington State University in 1939, and then studied at the St. Paul School of Art for two years (1939–40) before earning a master's degree from Columbia University (1941). In New York City, Feves's interest in ceramics flourished while working at a pottery shop and studying under Belarusian sculptor Ossip Zadkine at the Art Students League (1943). She married her husband, Dr. Louis Feves, in 1943, and moved with him to Pendleton, OR, following his tour of duty in WWII. In her home studio, which was well-equipped with kilns and potter's wheels, Feves explored several genres of ceramics, ranging from wall-mounted sculpture to slab and coil pots. Throughout her career, she emphasized the importance of an artist truly understanding the nature of his or her materials. Feves is represented in the collections of museums throughout the Northwest and California, including the Portland Art Museum and the Museum of Contemporary Craft in Portland, OR.

Bonfire Pot is one of several ceramic pots that Feves created as part of her Primitive Pottery series of the late 1970s and early '80s. Using a formula of equal parts plastic fireclay, local earthenware clay, and volcanic ash, Feves would handshape the clay to her desired result. Small circular patterns lining the top lip of this vessel were made by pressing a compact ball of clay against the surface. After being shaped, the pots were dried completely in the sun before being baked in a circular outdoor fire fueled by either wood or cow chips. The black splotches present on many of Feves's primitive pots, including *Bonfire Pot*, were created by hot cow chips clinging to the clay during firing; it was just this sort of unpredictable element that the artist appreciated.[1]

Schnitzer was enthusiastic and unwavering in her support of artists working in varied three-dimensional media, from ceramics to wood to steel. Along with Feves, Robert Arneson, and Mel Katz, the Fountain Gallery represented such talented artists as Tom Coleman, James Lee Hansen, Manuel Izquierdo, Lee Kelly, Tom Morandi, Hilda Morris, Ken Shores, and Donald Wilson.

1 "Betty W. Feves (1918–1985): A Collection," http://www.feves.com/betty/. Accessed March 28, 2012.

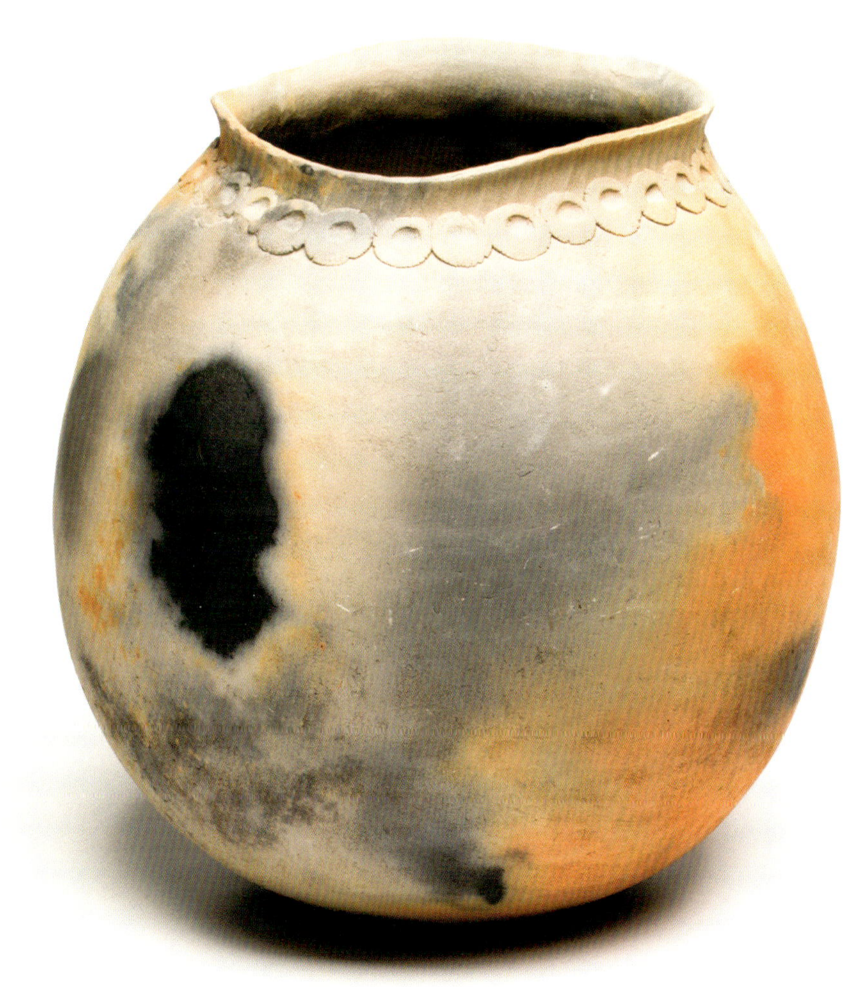

MORRIS GRAVES

(b. 1910, Fox Valley, OR; d. 2001, Loleta, CA)

Brazilian Screamers, 1931

Oil on canvas, 42 x 42 inches

PROVENANCE

Collection of George Arnold (1948)

Collection of William and Violet Dominick (1962)

Collection of Arlene and Harold Schnitzer (May 11, 1970–)

EXHIBITION HISTORY

Palace of the Legion of Honor, San Francisco, CA (1948–59)

The Upsher Collection Show, Oakland Art Museum, CA (July 21–August 12, 1962)

Dalzell Hatfield Gallery, Los Angeles, CA (October 9–November 9, 1970)

Art of the Pacific Northwest: From the 1930s to the Present, National Collection of Fine Arts, Smithsonian Institution, Washington, DC (February 8–May 5, 1974); traveled to Seattle Art Museum, WA (July 12–August 25, 1974), and Portland Art Museum, OR (September 17–October 13, 1974)

Morris Graves: The Early Works, Museum of Northwest Art, La Conner, WA (June 25–September 30, 1998); traveled to Greenville County Museum of Art, SC (March 17–May 16, 1999); Art Museum of Southeast Texas, Beaumont (September 9-November 30, 1999)

Morris Graves: Paintings, 1931–97, Whitney Museum of American Art, New York, NY (March 12–June 3, 1998)

Morris Graves achieved national recognition as a painter who infused scenes of natural subject matter—most frequently birds—with a mystical and intimate sensibility. Graves was largely self-taught as an artist. The Seattle Art Museum mounted his first, well-received show (1936), which resulted in his employment as an easel painter for the Federal Art Project of the Works Progress Administration (1936–39). He was featured in the important exhibition *Americans 1942* at the Museum of Modern Art that year. After the exposure of the MoMA exhibition, Graves held solo shows at the Detroit Art Institute (1943) and the Los Angeles County Museum of Art (1948). In 1964, after years of international travel, he settled down in rural Loleta, CA. There he purchased a 200-acre plot of redwood forest he named "The Lake," which remained his home and source of painting inspiration until his death at age ninety in 2001.

When Schnitzer acquired *Brazilian Screamers*, she asked Graves for an explanation of the cryptic embedded letters in the painting. Graves's letter to Schnitzer of April 26, 1971, offered this response: "The 'MLCCM' with the signature was some kind of code–initials for a highly personal comment–a religious juvenile conscience which served to both comment on the shortcomings (the failure) of the painting & ask forgiveness for indulging the sensuality of the act of painting. At that time I signed all paintings with some devised humility code! A protestant puritanical 'hang up' the feeling of which (strange!!) I have never really quite wholly gotten free of."[1] Schnitzer mused over *Brazilian Screamers*, "I've always wondered if by any chance he was at the zoo."[2] In this scene of flora and fauna, undulating lines and bold, contrasting colors create an hallucinogenic impression. Graves wrote of the painting that his subject was simply foliage, "vigorous luxuriant tropical plants . . . dominated by *sturdy* lines."[3]

1 Personal letter, Morris Graves to Arlene Schnitzer, April 26, 1971.

2 Interview with Schnitzer, September 15, 2011.

3 Personal letter, Morris Graves to Helen Graves, October 27, 1931.

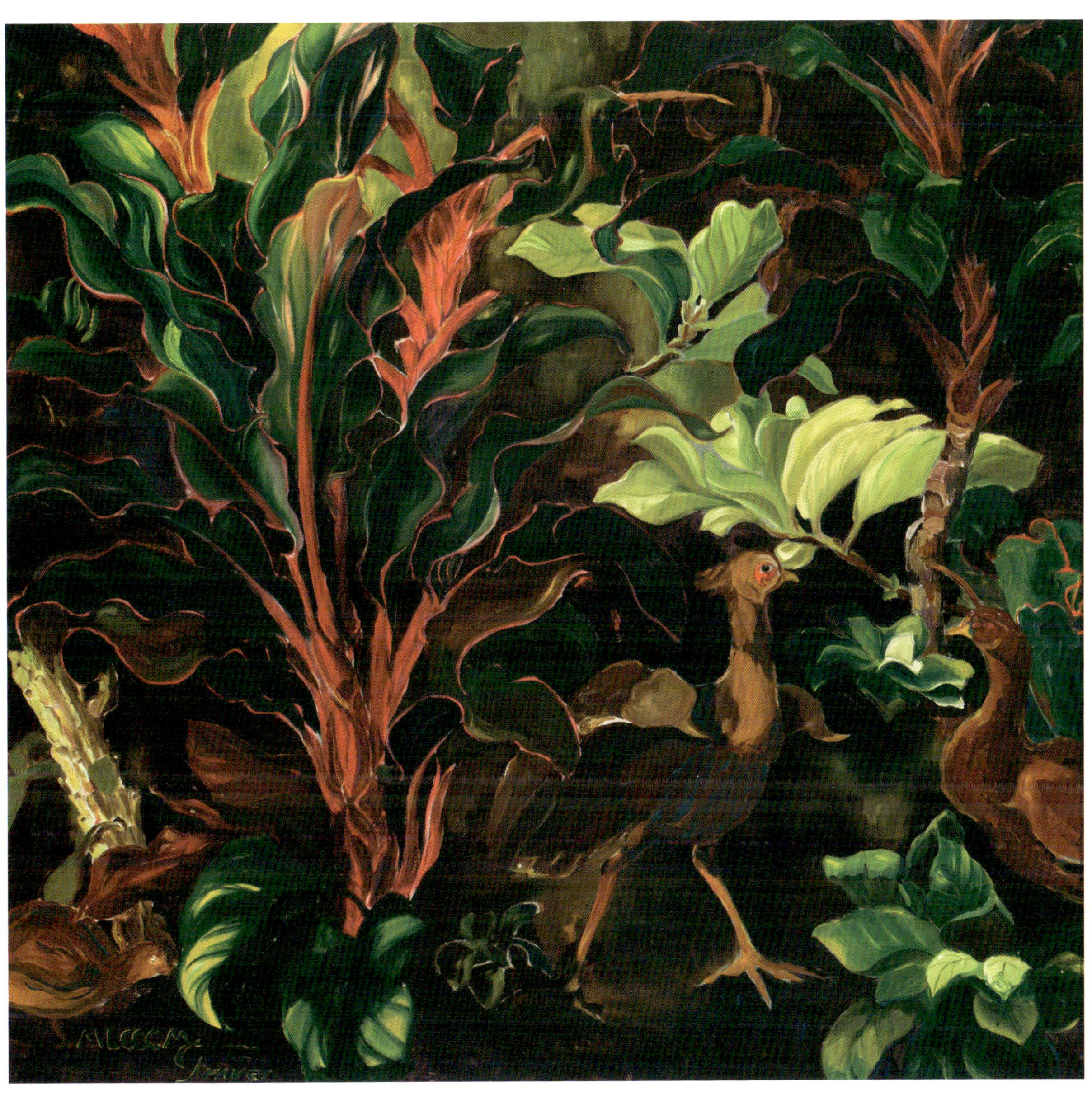

GREGORY GRENON

(b. 1948, Detroit, MI; currently lives in Portland, OR)

Ballerina, 2007

Oil on glass, 40 x 28 inches

PROVENANCE

Laura Russo Gallery, Portland, OR (2007)

Collection of Arlene and Harold Schnitzer (April 4, 2007–)

EXHIBITION HISTORY

Life is an Awkward Dance, Laura Russo Gallery, Portland, OR (April 5–28, 2007)

Portland-artist Gregory Grenon aims to reveal truths about his subjects, primarily women, at this precise moment in history. Grenon has an arts training background in etching, lithography, and welding and earned degrees in English Literature and Business. While living in Chicago in the early 1970s, he worked as an assistant printer at Landfall Press and later credited this experience for teaching him about color—as well as ensuring that he would ultimately "be a painter, not a teacher or printer."[1] His luminous portrayals of women are painted in a shockingly bright palette on clear glass. These frequently intense portraits are tempered by the traditional folk-art tone of his chosen medium. In 1994, Grenon stated, "I don't paint women as you want them to be. And I don't paint women as they should be painted. I simply paint women as they are."[2]

Schnitzer was adamant about Grenon, whose work was shown at the Fountain Gallery in the 1980s. "[He] is very important to me," she affirmed.[3] Grenon's *Ballerina,* which depicts a raven-haired dancer poised *en pointe*, is at once both aggressive and accessible. Her self-possessed gaze—a unifying characteristic among most of Grenon's female protagonists—assures the viewer that she is in complete control of her seemingly precarious stance. With arms outstretched and hands braced against the wall, she appears ready to leap out from the painted interior in which she is balanced. The women of Grenon's portraits are typically assertive, almost confrontational, in their body language; this ability to engage with the viewer and provoke a strong reaction resonates throughout works by many artists in the Arlene and Harold Schnitzer art collection. When running the Fountain Gallery, Schnitzer was just as dedicated to showcasing artwork that made the audience feel something—positive or negative. So long as the work was eliciting some strong response, she was satisfied: "I just didn't want it when [viewers] were indifferent."[4]

1 "Gregory Grenon – Bio," http://www.gregorygrenon.com/Bio.htm. Accessed February 23, 2012.

2 "Gregory Grenon – Statement: The Unidentified Woman," http://www.gregorygrenon.com/Statement.htm. Accessed February 23, 2012.

3 Interview with Schnitzer, November 7, 2011.

4 Interview with Schnitzer, September 15, 2011.

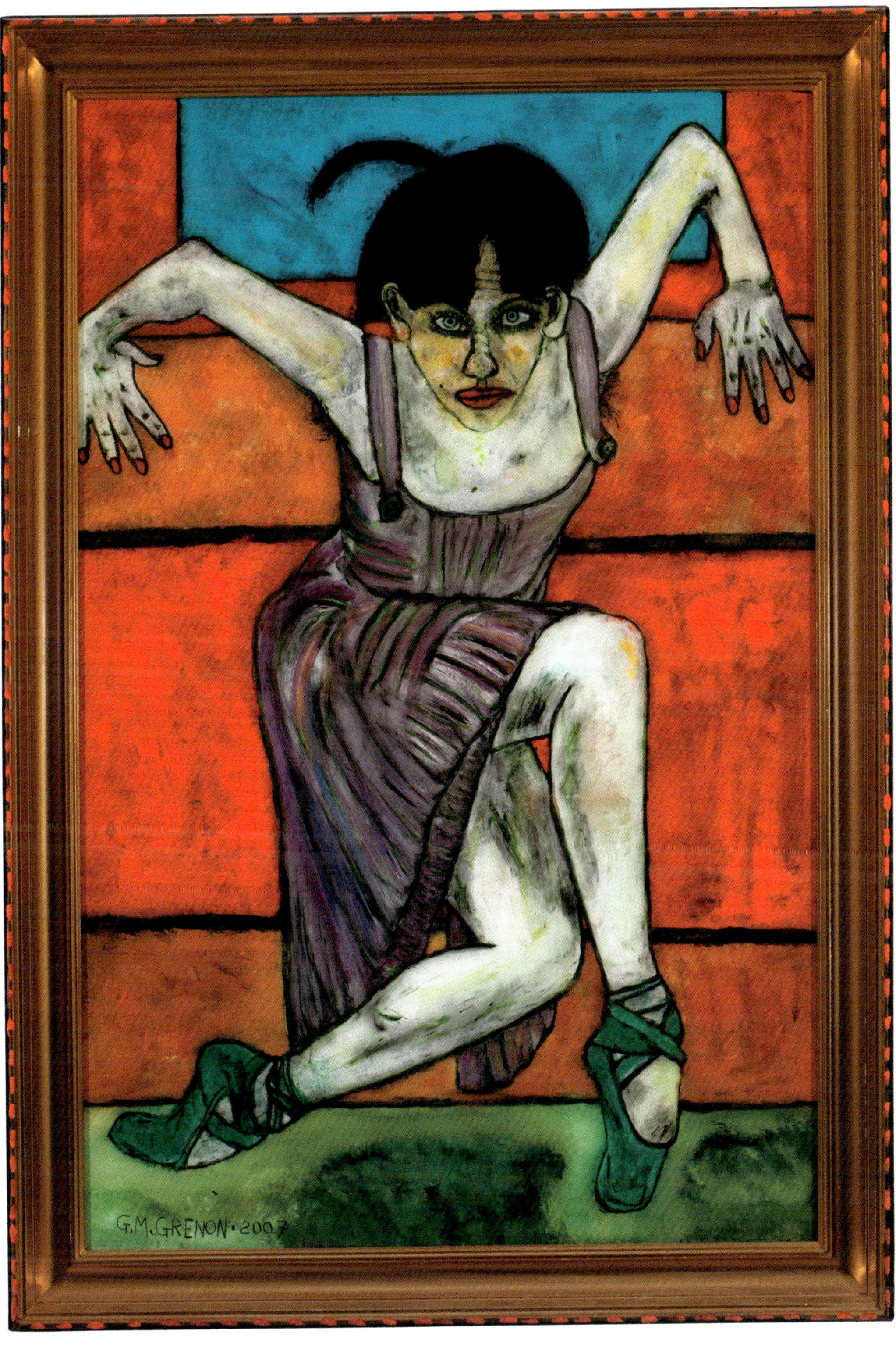
G.M.GRENON·2007

PAUL HORIUCHI

(b. 1906, Oishi, Yamanashi Prefecture, Japan;
d. 1999, Seattle, WA)

Forms in Red, 1961

Paper collage on canvas, 59 ¼ x 19 inches

PROVENANCE

The Fountain Gallery of Art, Portland, OR

Collection of Shirley Engleman

Collection of Arlene and Harold Schnitzer (May 18, 1989–)

Segments of Antiquity #2, 1984

Rice paper collage, 35 x 66 inches

PROVENANCE

The Fountain Gallery of Art, Portland, OR

Collection of Arlene and Harold Schnitzer

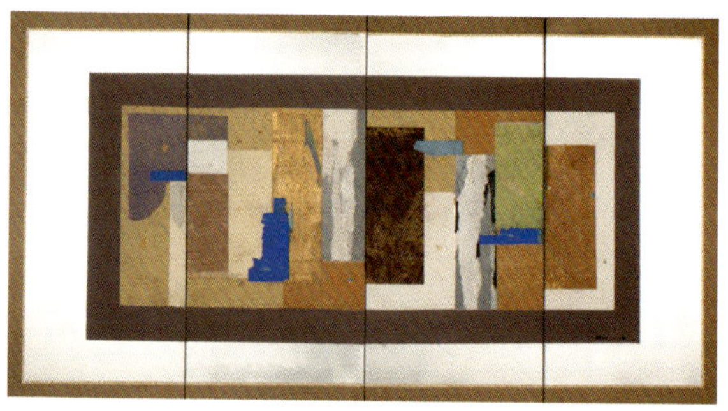

Paul Horiuchi's early art education in Japan consisted of classes in calligraphy, watercolor painting, and Sumi ink painting. After immigrating to the United States in 1920, he continued painting while employed by the Union Pacific railroad. The 1950s saw his first serious explorations into collage, the medium that he would ultimately master. Horiuchi's abstract, layered compositions were constructed from torn sheets of handmade paper, dyed in various pigments to achieve the desired palette, and assembled with a poetic appreciation for unexpected elements. He considered his process with torn paper to be the same as the process he used in painting. In 1956, Horiuchi's work was featured with three other Japanese-American artists (John Matsudaira, Kenjiro Nomura, and George Tsutakawa) at the Zoë Dusanne Gallery, the premier gallery for Northwest modern art in Seattle. That event was followed by his first solo museum exhibition at the Seattle Art Museum two years later. Though heavily influenced by the flatness of traditional Japanese art, Horiuchi was also particularly responsive to the work of Paul Cézanne, Vincent Van Gogh, Pablo Picasso, his close friend Mark Tobey, and the Abstract Expressionists. Among his many honors was his designation as a Sacred Treasure, Fourth Class, by the Emperor of Japan in 1976.

Forms in Red, a vertical collage on canvas, was sold to close friends of Arlene Schnitzer soon after the Fountain Gallery opened. It was when this artwork returned to her gallery decades later that she decided to purchase it for her own collection. Schnitzer was tuned into the cyclical nature of the art market and the ways in which artworks move through ownership—or stewardship, as she considers it—as collections and the collectors themselves change over time. She has a great respect for what Horiuchi accomplished in his career. "When you think about it, he really almost invented the torn rice paper collage bit. . . . He really did a phenomenal job with it. You know, it was just gorgeous."[1]

The collaged screen *Segments of Antiquity #2* represents a body of work by Horiuchi that makes a more obvious reference to his Asian background and the tradition of Japanese screen paintings. Along with their aesthetic appeal, Schnitzer recognized the marketable quality of these works, which she said practically "walked out the door" of the gallery: "I think he knew exactly what he was doing, by doing the screens. ... and that was part of him being so smart. He made them precious."[2]

1 Interview with Schnitzer, September 15, 2011

2 Ibid

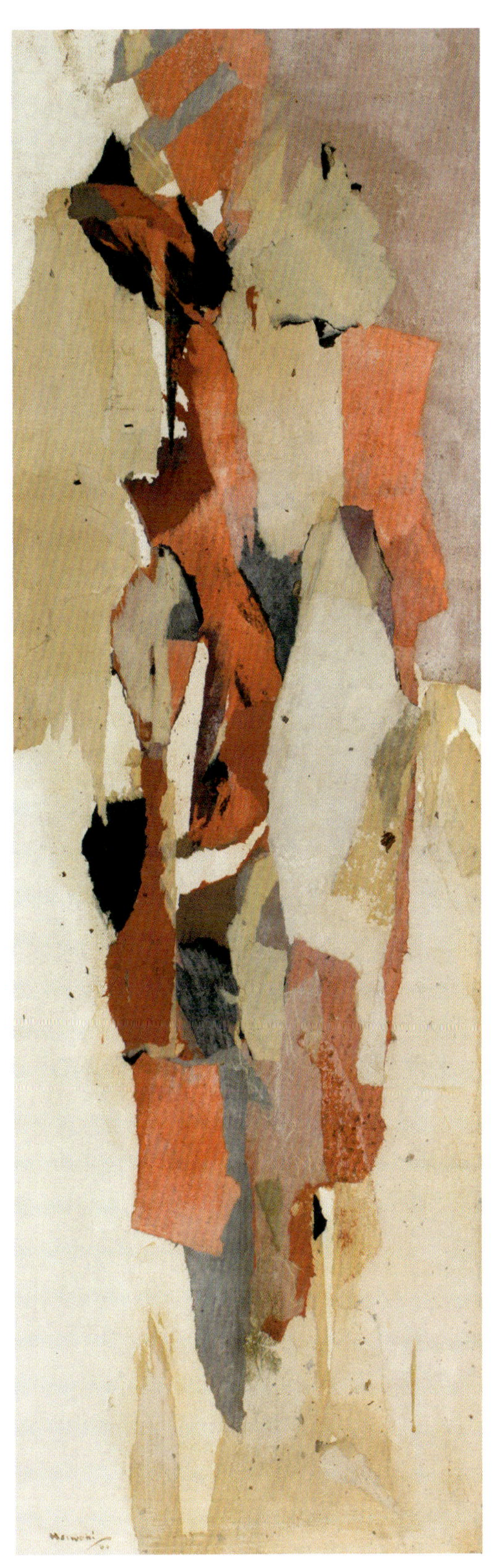

FAY JONES

(b. 1953, Boston, MA; currently lives in Seattle, WA)

Oasis, 1986

Acrylic and collage on paper, 39 x 53 ¼ inches

PROVENANCE

Laura Russo Gallery, Portland, OR (1988)

Collection of Arlene and Harold Schnitzer (March 1, 1989–)

EXHIBITION HISTORY

Personal Visions, Heathman Hotel, Portland, OR (September 20–November 22, 1993)

Born in 1936 in Boston, Fay Jones attended the Rhode Island School of Design, where she earned her BFA (1957). There, she met her husband, painter Robert Jones, and the two moved to Seattle in 1960 when he received a teaching position at the University of Washington. Jones is one of Seattle's most esteemed artists. She has numerous public artworks in the city, including her large painted ceramic murals in Westlake Station. Jones's work has been featured in more than 100 solo and group exhibitions and is included in the collections of the Boise Museum of Art, the Portland Art Museum, the Seattle Art Museum, and the Tacoma Art Museum. In 1997, the Boise Museum of Art held a twenty-year retrospective of her work.

Jones's paintings are visionary meditations, often containing animals and faces floating like mirages across an abstracted or surreal backdrop. In *Oasis,* mysterious figures clothed in vivid, colorful patterns are juxtaposed with two birds, whose bizarre, gravity-defying positions disorient the viewer and disrupt the scene. Each figure within the dreamscape seems oblivious of the others, and what each seeks in the oasis is left for the viewer to decide. Referring to her as an iconic Seattle painter, Schnitzer has said, "There's almost a cult around her."[1] Jones is among the group of regional artists whom Schnitzer has especially enjoyed observing as their careers evolved. "I love the artists, I love the art," she said. "Cindy Parker [has] been a great joy in my life, to watch her grow and develop . . . Greg Grenon, who walked into my life, who's fresh and creative and gutsy, and people from Seattle like Jack Chevalier, and Fay Jones, and this whole new crop of very serious young artists. . . . That's what art's all about."[2]

1 Interview with Schnitzer, November 5, 2011.

2 *Oral history interview with Arlene Schnitzer, conducted by Bruce Guenther, June 7–8, 1985. Archives of American Art, Smithsonian Institution.*

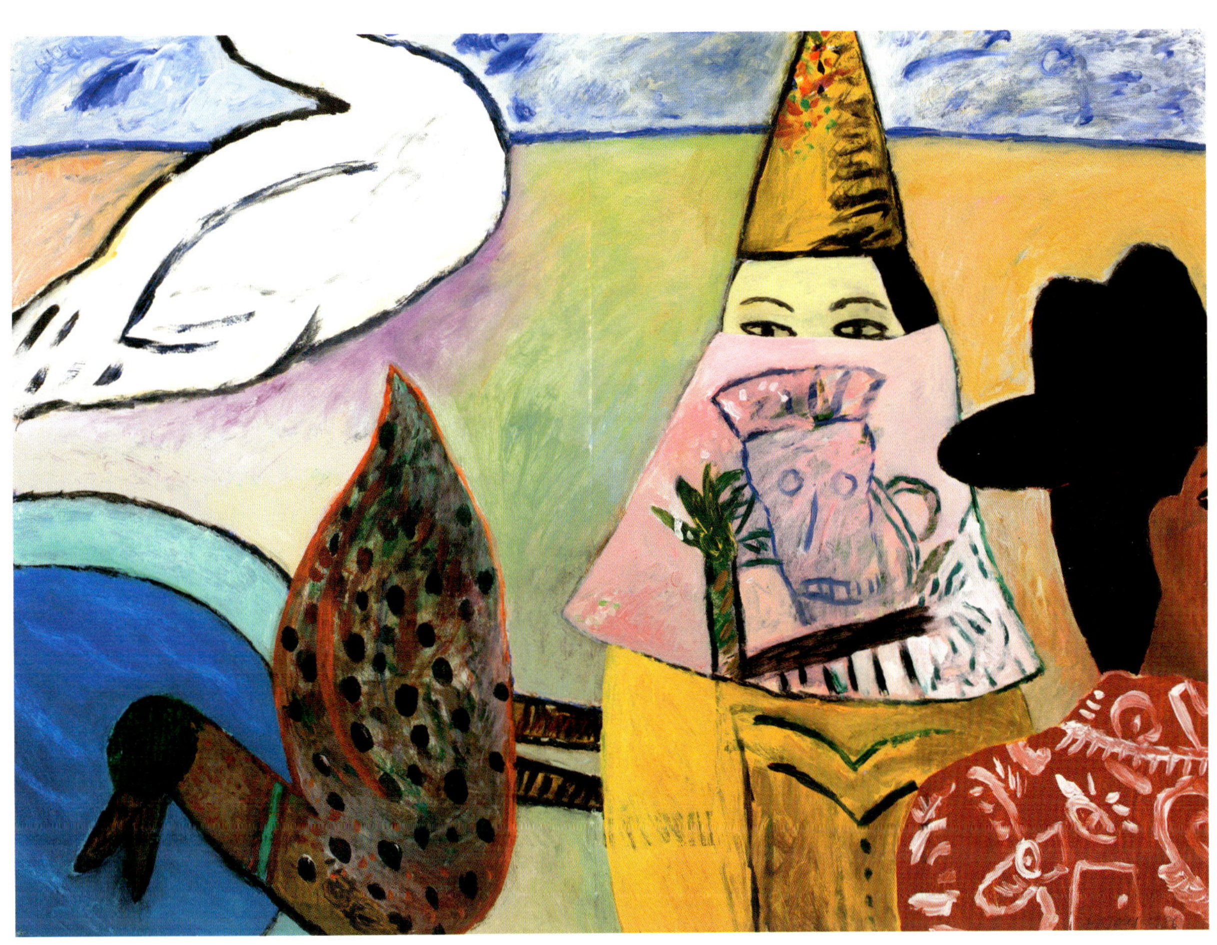

JUN KANEKO

(b. 1942, Nagoya, Japan; currently lives in Omaha, NE)

Plate #8, 1986

Ceramic, 26 x 20 ½ x 5 inches

PROVENANCE

Dorothy Weiss Gallery, San Francisco, CA

Collection of Arlene and Harold Schnitzer (September 16, 1988–)

Untitled Dango #5, 1986

Ceramic, 15 x 21 x 15 inches

PROVENANCE

Paul Klein Gallery, Chicago, IL

Collection of Arlene and Harold Schnitzer (September 16, 1988–)

EXHIBITION HISTORY

Jun Kaneko, Paul Klein Gallery, Chicago, IL (1988)

Portland Collects Contemporary Ceramics, Museum of Contemporary Craft, Portland, OR (January 14–March 6, 2005)

Jun Kaneko's work synthesizes painting and sculpture in a unique way, pushing the technical capacity of ceramics as a medium and maintaining an authorial presence. He is best known for the large-scale glazed ceramic pieces he refers to as "dango" sculptures (*dango* means "rounded form" in Japanese). Kaneko studied painting from an early age, working in an artist studio during the day and attending high school in the evenings. He came to the United States in 1963 to continue his education at the Chouinard Institute of Art in Los Angeles, where he studied ceramics under Peter Voulkos. Kaneko would later teach at the University of New Hampshire (1972–73), Scripps College (1974), the Rhode Island School of Design (1973–75), and Cranbrook Academy of Art (1979–86). He received an honorary doctorate from the Royal College of Art in London (2005). His exhibition history spans forty years, and his works are included in collections at Cranbrook, the De Young Museum, the Detroit Institute of Art, the European Ceramic Work Centre, the Fine Art Museum of San Francisco, Oakland Museum, the Philadelphia Museum of Art, the Smithsonian's Renwick Gallery, and Japan's Wakayama Museum of Modern Art.

Plate #8 belongs to a specific category of Jun Kaneko's work: oval ceramic plates of commensurable size, decorated with abstract patterning. The artist disrupts a steady rhythm of lines with three discrete decorative elements, placing a prominent curlicue at the center. The piece seems rusticated in its color and simple ornament, and thus it evokes an artistic period much earlier than Kaneko's own.

Untitled Dango #5 represents Jun Kaneko's most characteristic form. The "dango" appears as if wrapped by a black-and-white ribbon that, aside from overlapping, continues unbroken along the work's surface. His decorative technique unifies the composition and also plays with ideas of concealment.

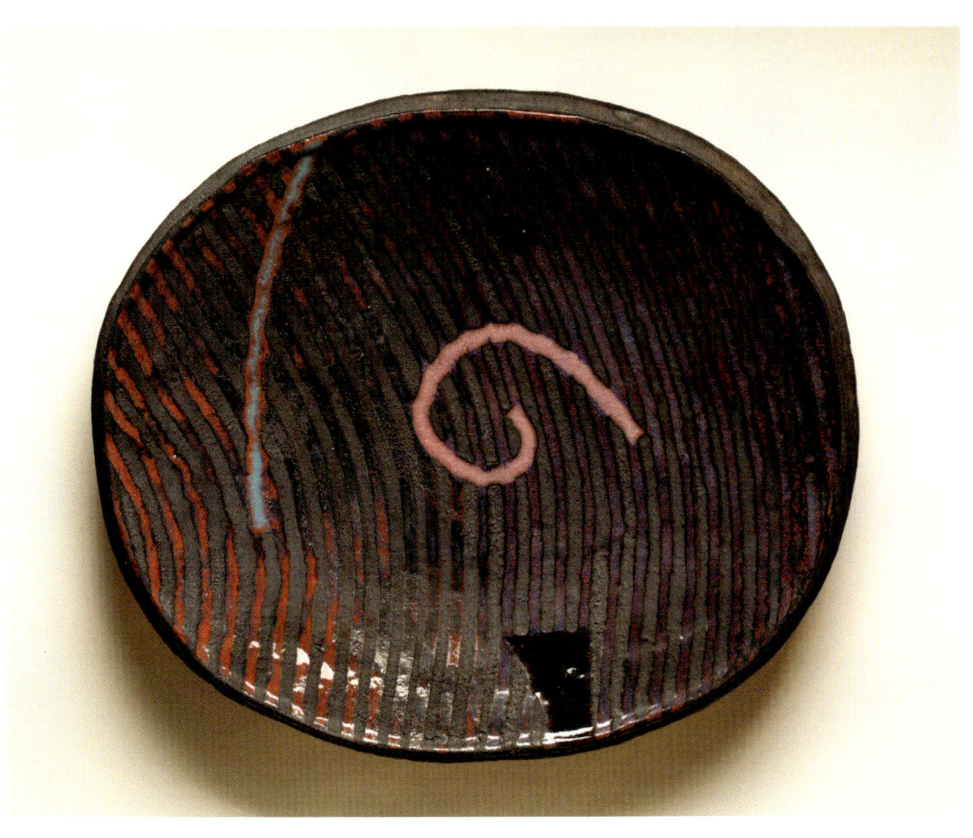

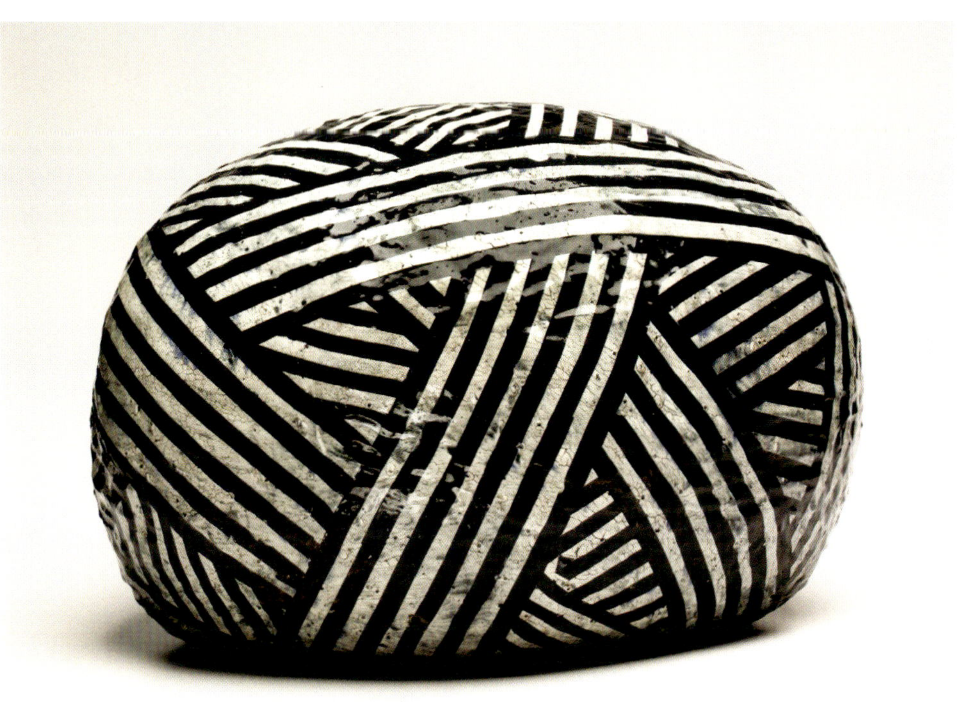

MEL KATZ

(b. 1932, Brooklyn, NY; currently lives in Portland)

Still Life (Model), 2006

Painted aluminum, 29 x 12 ¾ x 6 inches

PROVENANCE

Laura Russo Gallery, Portland, OR (2006–10)

Collection of Arlene and Harold Schnitzer (February 17, 2010–)

EXHIBITION HISTORY

20th Anniversary Gallery Group Show, Laura Russo Gallery, Portland, OR (October 2006)

PNCA Benefit Art Auction, Pacific Northwest College of Art, Portland, OR (February 17, 2010)

New York native Mel Katz attended the Brooklyn Museum Art School from 1954 to 1955 and moved to Portland in 1964 to take a position teaching at the Portland Art Museum. The following year, when Robert Colescott went on sabbatical from his teaching position at Portland State University to study at the American Research Center in Cairo, Egypt, Katz took over his classes, and in 1972, he founded the Portland Center for the Visual Arts with fellow artists Michele Russo and Jay Backstrand. Initially a painter, Katz became increasingly interested in sculpture. The three-dimensional works for which he's best known are intrinsically tied to his mastery of two dimensionality and the basic elements of design. All of his work, Katz declares, is determined by his media, with "line always in the forefront."[1] After designing the specifications for a new sculpture, the plans are fabricated in metalworking shops using materials such as steel, aluminum, or Formica.

Katz's *Still Life (Model),* with its mix of organic and architectural elements, encapsulates those qualities that typify his prolific body of work. The artist described *Still Life (Model)* as being more "real" than much of his other work, in that it references recognizable subject matter—in this case, a still life set up on a table—in a more obvious way. However, the principles that have directed Katz's art-making are just as present here, with the sharply defined geometric shapes and bold, eye-popping color. When Katz first met Schnitzer, in the 1960s, he was still concentrating on painting. Her first visit to his studio came during a period of experimentation with a very subdued palette, which Katz recalls prompted Schnitzer to exclaim, "Where's the color?"[2]

1 Interview with Mel Katz by Lawrence Fong and Danielle Knapp, Portland, OR. January 19, 2012.

2 Ibid

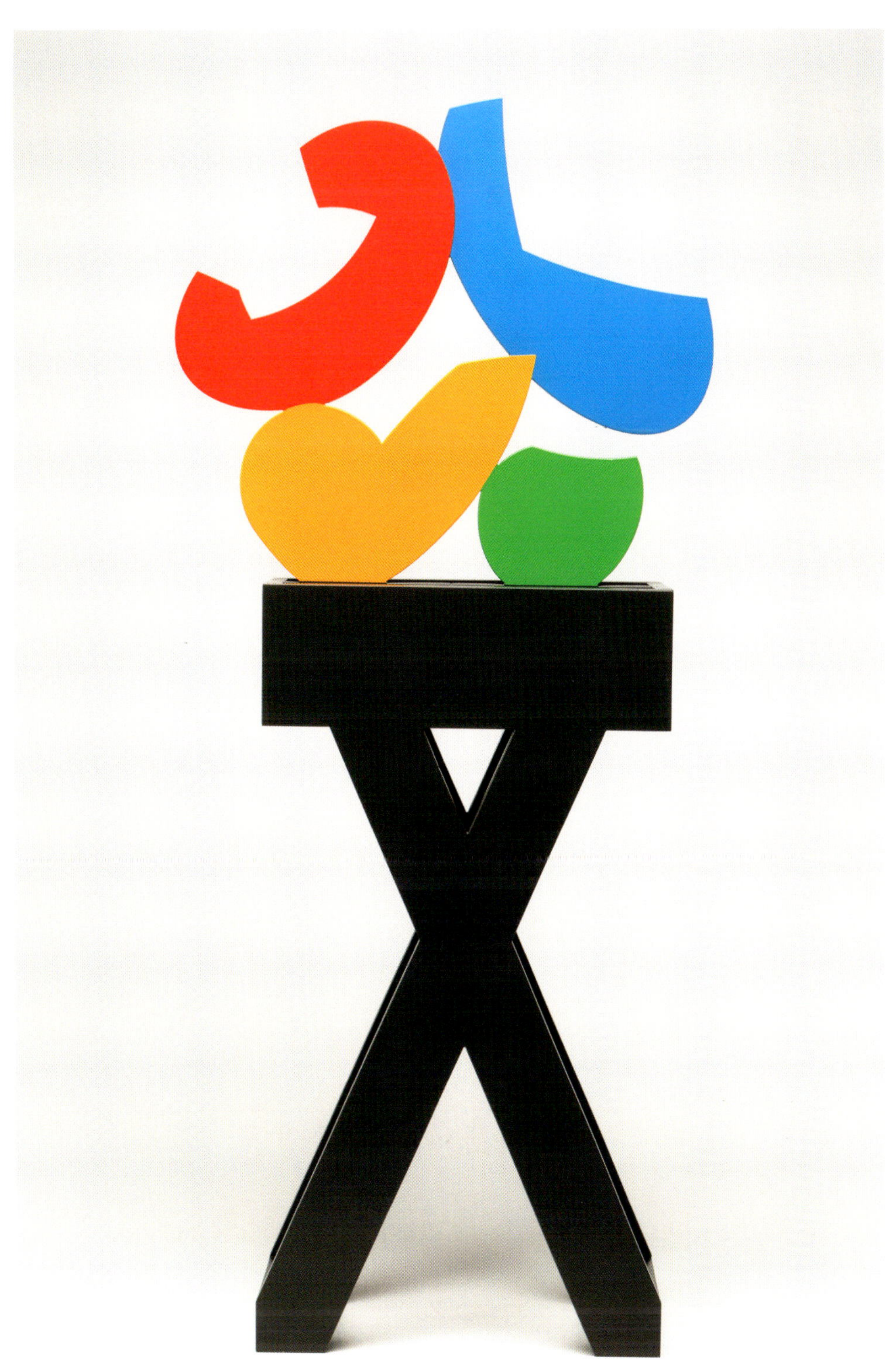

STANISLAV LIBENSKÝ and JAROSLAVA BRYCHTOVÁ

(b. 1921, Sezemice, Czechoslovakia; d. 2002, Železný Brod, Czech Republic)

(b. 1924, Železný Brod, Czechoslovakia; currently lives in Železný Brod, Czech Republic)

Rhomboid Head, 1991

Cast glass, 19 ½ x 22 x 11 inches

PROVENANCE

Heller Gallery, New York, NY (1991–1993)

Collection of Arlene and Harold Schnitzer (October 9, 1993–)

EXHIBITION HISTORY

Heller Gallery, New York, NY (1993)

Stanislav Libenský and Jaroslava Brychtová are often credited with transforming the field of glass making from craft to fine art. The two artists were inseparable collaborators until Libenský's death in 2002 and stand as towering figures in the realm of glass art. Libenský studied at the Specialized School of Glassmaking in Novy Bor and Železný Brod in the Czech Republic from 1937 to 1939, and then at the School of Applied Arts in Prague from 1939 to 1944. In 1953, he returned to Železný Brod to become the director of the Specialized School of Glassmaking, where he met Brychtová, the daughter of the school's co-founder, Jaroslav Brychta. Brychtová had been experimenting with casting and carving glass since the late 1940s and founded the Center for Architectural Glass at the Specialized School of Glassmaking. Of their meeting, Libenský remembered, "When I came to Železný Brod, I made a drawing of a head that was shaped like a bowl. Ms. Brychtová came and said, 'Mr. Libenský, may I turn this drawing into something three-dimensional?' I said, 'Yes, try it,' and she tried so successfully that we continued to work together. It worked because I trained as a painter and she trained as a sculptor."[1]

This translation between media was the central feature of the pair's collaborative process. Libenský began by making line drawings in pen or pencil and, then, colored sketches in charcoal and tempera. Brychtová created a clay model based upon the drawings, which was cast in plaster to make a mold for the glass. Libenský explained, "When you have only one author, that person makes a drawing, makes a mold, and so on. There is only one line of thought. When you have two people working together, you can come back and develop the idea, pushing it further."[2] Brychtová brought the concept from the drawing into what the artists call the "light-space" dimension, in which the medium of glass has a unique capacity for expression. In works like *Rhomboid Head*, Libenský and Brychtová reduced figurative elements to their most basic geometric forms, transforming these forms into Cubist-influenced optical experiences. In response to a question about the temporality of their work, Brychtová noted, "Glass makes it possible to see the whole sculptural form from one point of view. The Cubists wanted to make everything visible from one point of view, and that's something that glass does quite naturally."[3]

1 Peter S. Green, "Stanislav Libenský, 80; Redefined Glass Art," *The New York Times*, March 2, 2002. http://www.nytimes.com/2002/03/02/arts/stanislav-libensky-80-redefined-glass-art.html. Accessed February 28, 2012.

2 Robert Kehlmann, *The Inner Light: Sculpture by Stanislav Libenský and Jaroslava Brychtová* (Washington: Museum of Glass, 2002), 73.

3 Robert Kehlmann, *The Inner Light*, 77.

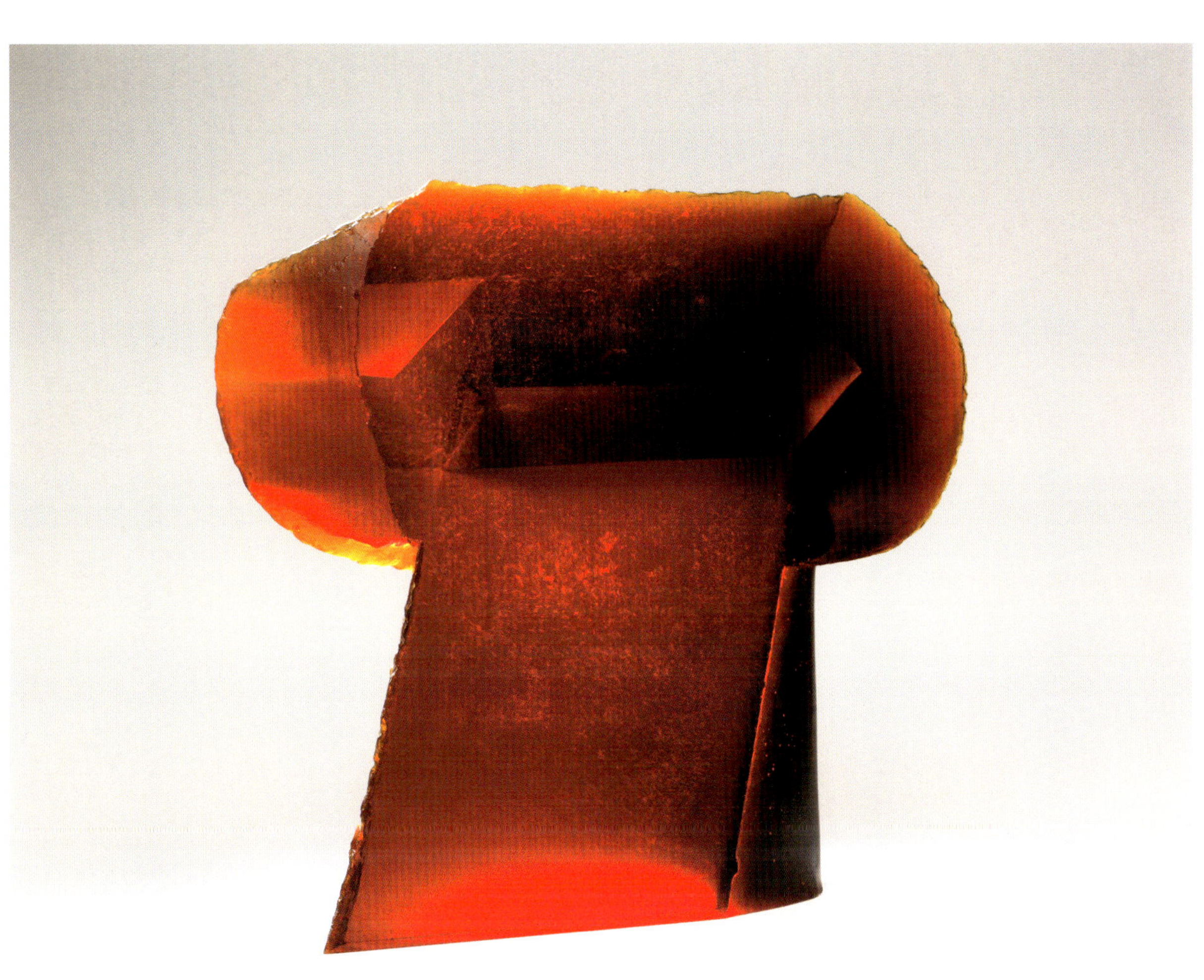

SHERRY MARKOVITZ

(b. 1947, Chicago, IL; currently lives in Seattle, WA)

Shine on Me, 2002–2006

Glass beads, papier-mâché, found objects, mixed media, 38 x 18 x 16 inches

PROVENANCE

Greg Kucera Gallery, Seattle, WA (2006)

Collection of Arlene and Harold Schnitzer (August 13, 2009–)

EXHIBITION HISTORY

Shimmer—Paintings and Sculptures 1979–2007, Museum of Art, Washington State University, Pullman (February 22–April 12, 2008); Bellevue Art Museum, WA (May 15–September 7, 2008); Schneider Museum of Art, Southern Oregon University, Ashland, OR (September 25–December 13, 2008)

Contrasts: A Glass Primer, Museum of Glass, Tacoma, WA (January–November 9, 2009)

Sherry Markovitz received her BA in Ceramics and Art Education from the University of Wisconsin, Madison (1969), and her MFA in Printmaking from the University of Washington (1975). Markovitz works in drawing, painting, and sculpture, weaving continuous themes throughout her different media. Her sculptures are painstakingly assembled by hand, layered with a shimmering decorative surface of glass beads and found objects that takes years to complete. She has received grants and awards from such organizations as the Washington Arts Commission and the Seattle Arts Commission, and her work is in many public collections, including the Museum of Arts and Design in New York, the Seattle Art Museum, and the Tacoma Art Museum.

Markovitz's work makes use of a rich body of associations, from folk art, ecology and mysticism to feminism and Surrealism, and her process has been described as "excessive," "extravagant," "dazzling," and "delirious."[1] The remarkably elaborate facture of her sculptures, combined with the abundance of cultural and psychological references, certainly merits all those adjectives. Schnitzer was immediately dazzled by *Shine on Me* when she saw it exhibited at Tacoma's Museum of Glass, saying, "I just made a beeline for it. I couldn't believe it was available, I mean, my God!"[2] In *Shine on Me*, Markovitz seems to be referencing a diverse range of global art cultures, from the pale creamy face of Russian dolls to the colorful patterns and animal imagery of Native American textiles. She used tiny translucent beads for the flesh and placed mirrors on the hands and dress to emphasize the doll's relationship to light. Schnitzer credits her husband, Harold, for the ingenious display of this piece in their home: he had the idea to place a mirror under the doll, which allows viewers a full appreciation of the work's ornate embellishment.[3]

1 Sherry Markovitz, Chris Bruce, and Josine Ianco-Starrels, *Sherry Markovitz: Shimmer Paintings and Sculptures, 1979-2007* (Pullman: Museum of Art/Washington State University, 2008), 18-19.

2 Interview with Schnitzer, September 15, 2011.

3 Ibid

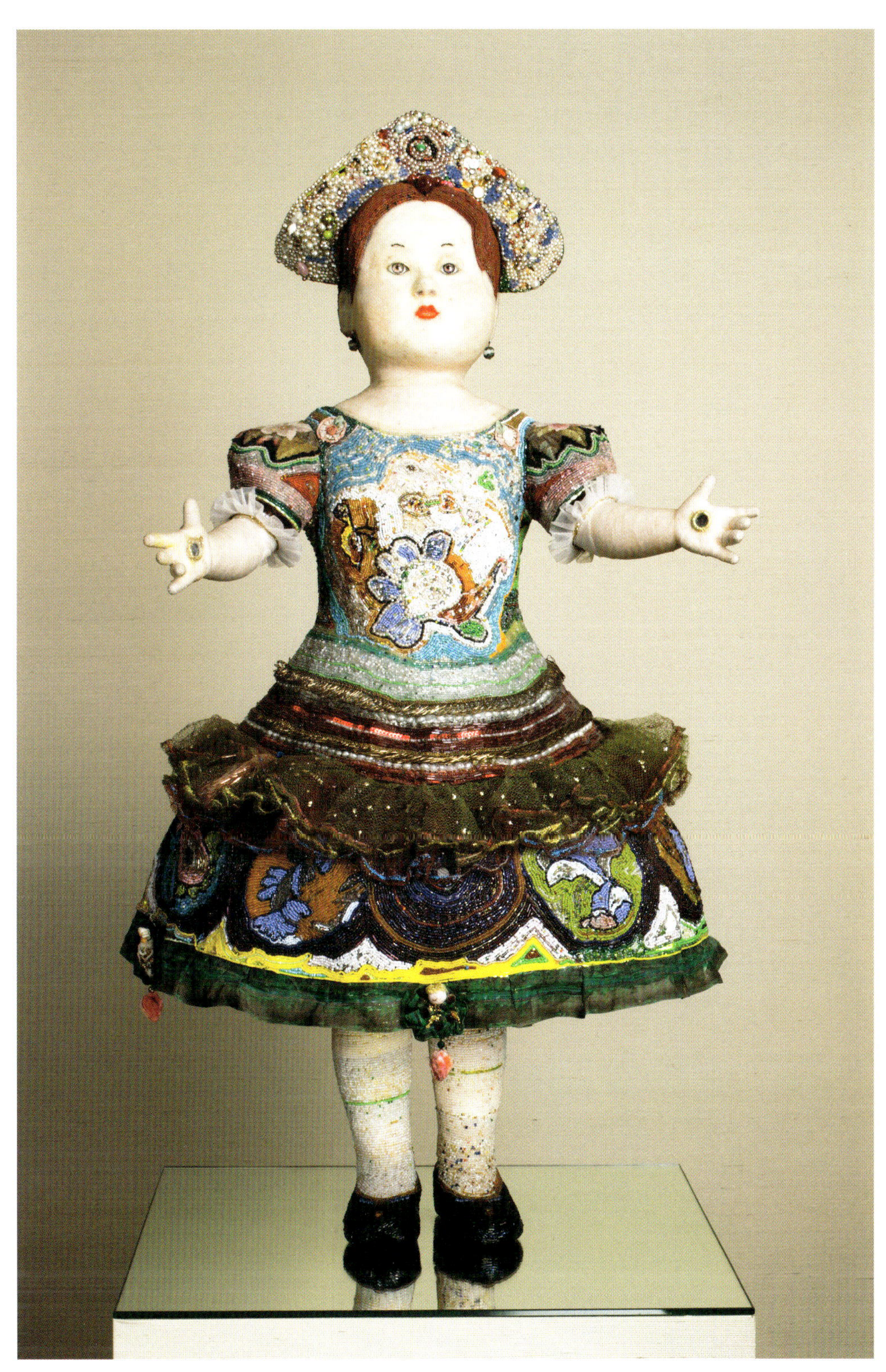

CARL MORRIS

(b. 1911, Yorba Linda, CA; d. 1993, Portland, OR)

Journey, 1946

Oil on heavy cardboard, 12 ½ x 24 ½ inches

PROVENANCE

Collection of Erma Bert Nelson

Collection of Arlene and Harold Schnitzer (March 28, 1983–)

EXHIBITION HISTORY

Carl Morris: History of Religions, Jordan Schnitzer Museum of Art, University of Oregon, Eugene, OR (June 30–September 9, 2007)

Carl Morris: Figure, Word and Light, The Art Gym, Marylhurst University, Lake Oswego, OR (January 13–February 13, 2008)

Art and People: Spokane Art Center and the Great Depression, Northwest Museum of Arts and Culture, Spokane, WA (November 14, 2009–April 10, 2010)

Carl Morris is one of Oregon's most acclaimed painters; in a career spanning over fifty years he achieved a national reputation with numerous exhibitions and awards, and his work is in such public collections as the Art Institute of Chicago, the Hirshhorn Collection at the National Gallery of Art, the Metropolitan Museum of Art, the San Francisco Museum of Art, and the Smithsonian. He began his art education at the School of the Art Institute of Chicago in 1931 and in 1933 was awarded a scholarship to study at the Akadamie der Bildenen Künste in Vienna. Morris spent two years in Austria and one studying in Paris at the Institute for International Education, gaining exposure to the major trends of avant-garde European painting. Upon returning to the U.S., Morris taught briefly at the Art Institute of Chicago and then worked in the Northwest for the WPA, fulfilling commissions for murals (including *Agriculture* and *Lumbering* at the Eugene Post Office in 1941), teaching, and creating smaller figural works. In 1959, he received a commission to paint a series of nine murals for the Hall of the History of Religions at the Oregon Centennial Exposition in Portland. Though Morris remained in Oregon for the rest of his life, he never abandoned his New York connections.

Morris has been identified with both the school of "Northwest Mystic" artists that included his close friend Mark Tobey and the New York School of Abstract Expressionist painters, such as Mark Rothko and Barnett Newman.[1]

Journey is emblematic of Morris's style in the mid-1940s, in which solid but luminescent figures inhabit a dark, shifting landscape. As Schnitzer prepared to open the Fountain Gallery, Morris provided invaluable guidance, making several recommendations of artists she should consider representing. His and Hilda's home in Portland was a regular gathering place for members of the creative and intellectual community. "You'd sit up there late at night at their house and have a drink or two, and boy, I want to tell you, they got into the most esoteric, philosophically abstract conversations," Schnitzer remembered. It was this camaraderie and the lifestyle available to artists working in the region that Schnitzer identified as the reason so many talented painters and sculptors were compelled to stay: "Why does everybody come back? It draws you. It's the Northwest. It pulls you back. Why did Carl stay? Why did Hilda stay? . . . This lifestyle seduces you. You don't leave. And this isn't just the visual artist. This is the musician, the actor, and everything."[2]

1 Prudence Roberts, *Carl Morris: Figure, Word & Light* (Marylhurst, OR: The Art Gym, Marylhurst University, 2008).

2 Interview with Schnitzer, September 15, 2011.

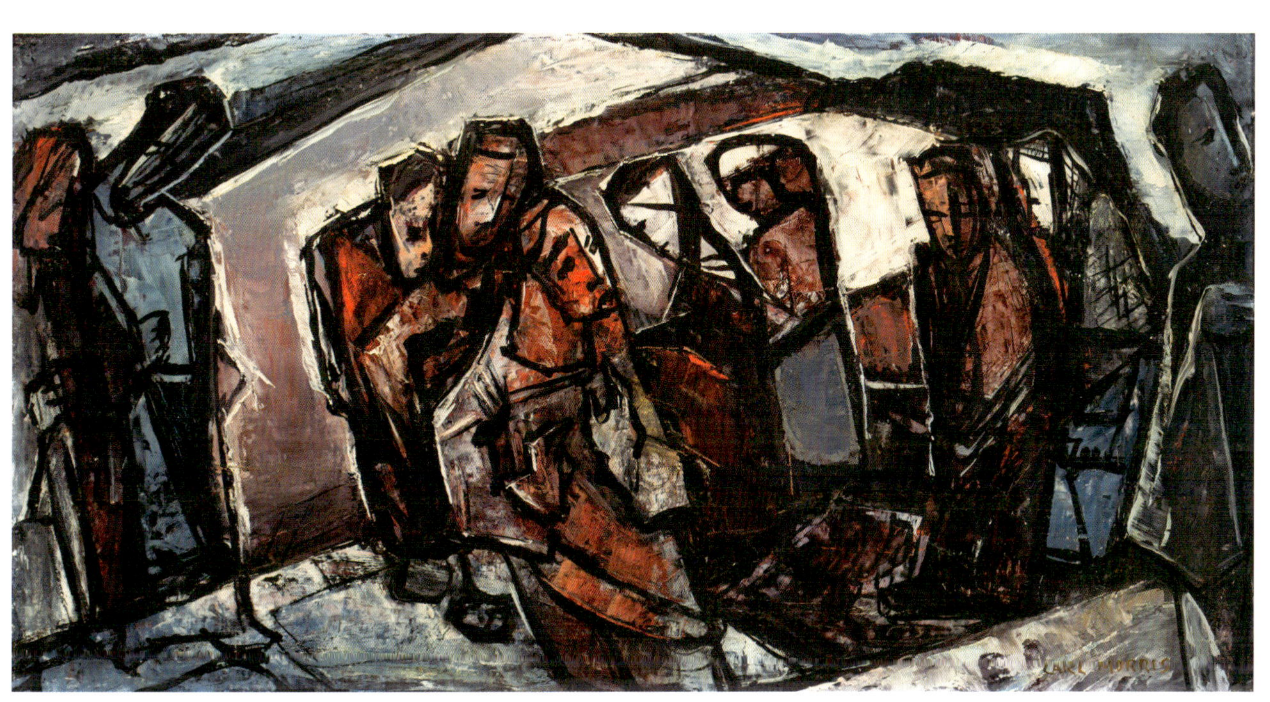

WILLIAM MORRIS

(b. 1957, Carmel, CA; currently lives in Stanwood, WA)

Medicine Jar (Corn and Horse), 2005

Blown glass, 14 x 7 x 24 inches

PROVENANCE

Imago Galleries, Palm Desert, CA (2005–06)

Collection of Arlene and Harold Schnitzer (January 31, 2006–)

William Morris studied ceramics at California State University and Central Washington University. In 1978, he began taking classes at the Pilchuck Glass School (meanwhile, working as a driver for the school to pay his tuition), the start of a long relationship with the institution that would ultimately include his serving as a gaffer, teacher, artist in residence, artistic director (1991), and a member of the board of directors (1992). His ten-year apprenticeship under master glassmaker Dale Chihuly, which Morris started while enrolled at Pilchuck, was instrumental in his training.

Archeological research and mythology, interests that began early in his life as he became familiar with Native American history in his hometown of Carmel, inform his artistic practice. Morris's work is especially impressive because of its surface quality, which frequently eschews the expected elements of glass—its characteristic transparency and shine—in favor of mimicking the natural texture of the subjects. He can manipulate blown glass to convincingly resemble such materials as bone, wood, stone, or fiber. Works by Morris are included in the collections of such museums as the American Craft Museum, the Louvre, the Metropolitan Museum of Art, the Musée des Arts Decoratifs in Paris, and the Victoria and Albert Museum.

Medicine Jar (Corn and Horse) is a functional vessel composed of a frosted, richly textured hollow corncob, embellished with the image of a cow, on which a small seated horse—that serves as the jar's stopper—is balanced. By titling the sculpture (and many others in his body of work), Morris has placed it squarely in the category of the ritual cultural object, though typically his medicine jars are so elaborately embellished that their purpose is not immediately recognizable to viewers. Morris's series have included "canopic jars" in the tradition of Egyptian cinerary urns, enigmatic forms based on animal and organic shapes that he calls "artifacts," and bulbous "fish traps" that appear to be wrapped in netting instead of the actual strands of blown glass.

The Arlene and Harold Schnitzer art collection includes many glass sculptures by such talented contemporary artists as Emily Brock, Dale Chihuly, Preston Singletary, and Therman Statom, but Morris, by whom Schnitzer owns several works, is a particular favorite.

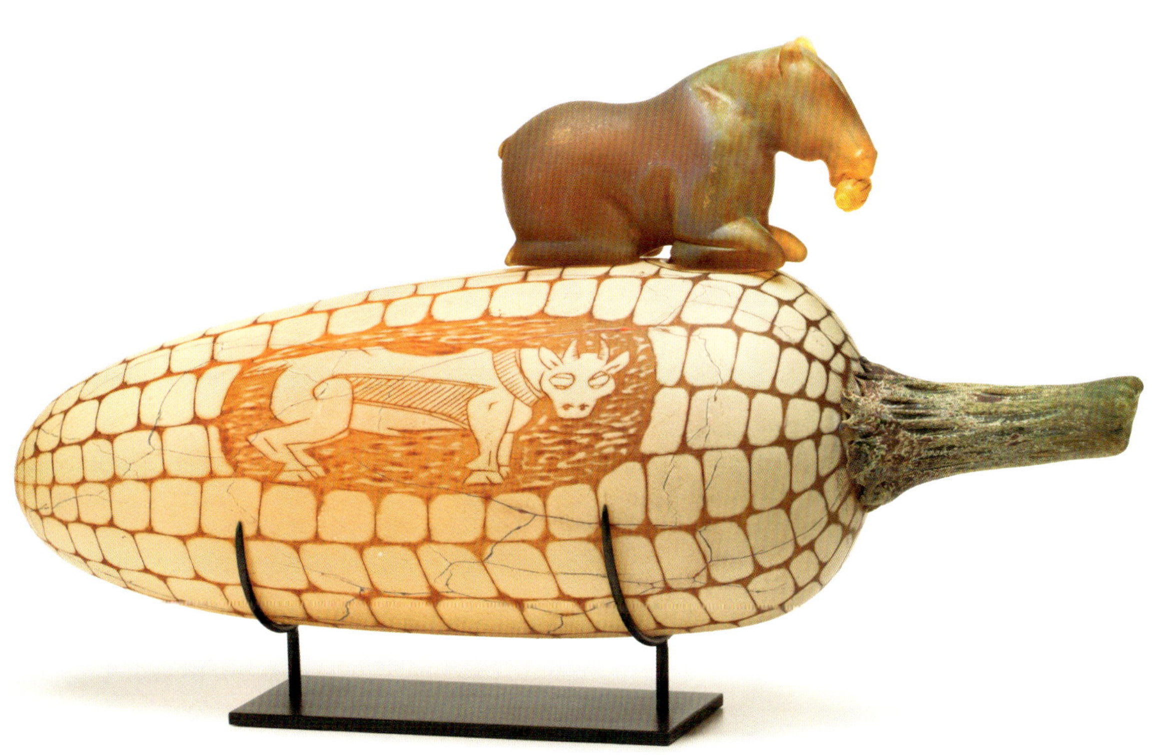

DEBORAH OROPALLO

(b. 1954, Hackensack, NJ; currently lives in San Francisco, CA)

Bride (Angel), 2007

Pigment print on Hahnemuhle 310g paper, 60 x 40 inches

Edition 2 of 10

PROVENANCE

Greg Kucera Gallery, Seattle, WA (June 7, 2007)

Collection of Arlene and Harold Schnitzer (June 7, 2007–)

EXHIBITIONS

Guise, Greg Kucera Gallery, Seattle, WA (June 7–June 30, 2007)

Deborah Oropallo received her BFA from Alfred University in 1979, followed by an MA and an MFA from the University of California, Berkeley, in 1982 and 1983, respectively. Oropallo's work fuses art historical material with contemporary photography and digital manipulation, exploring the aesthetic and conceptual possibilities of hybridized media. As she has described it, "I use the computer as the tool, but painting is the language of deliberation that is running through my head. I do not want to just repaint an illustration of what the computer can do, but to push the pixels themselves as paint, and to layer imagery and veils to create depth and volume. Like painting, this process can engage nuance and subtlety. It also has the ability to alter an image in a way that no other medium can deliver or predict."[1]

Oropallo's *Bride (Angel),* is from *Guise*, a suite of fifteen prints created in 2007. In this series, Oropallo layered seventeenth-and eighteenth-century portraiture with images of women in revealing Halloween costumes. Conflating the image of an aristocrat flaunting his wealth and power with that of young women displaying their sexuality creates an ironically humorous creature. However, to suggest that there are only these two layers would do an injustice, for the piece is intricately composed and manipulated to both seduce and perplex the eye. *Bride (Angel)* raises questions of the relationship between portraiture and voyeurism and between power and sexuality. Oropallo's unique process creates a subtle and visually enchanting puzzle for the viewer in which the effort of extracting a singular narrative is foiled by a multiplicity of ideas and sensations.

1 "Guise: Suite of Nineteen Prints," http://www.gregkucera.com/oropallo.htm. Accessed March 12, 2012.

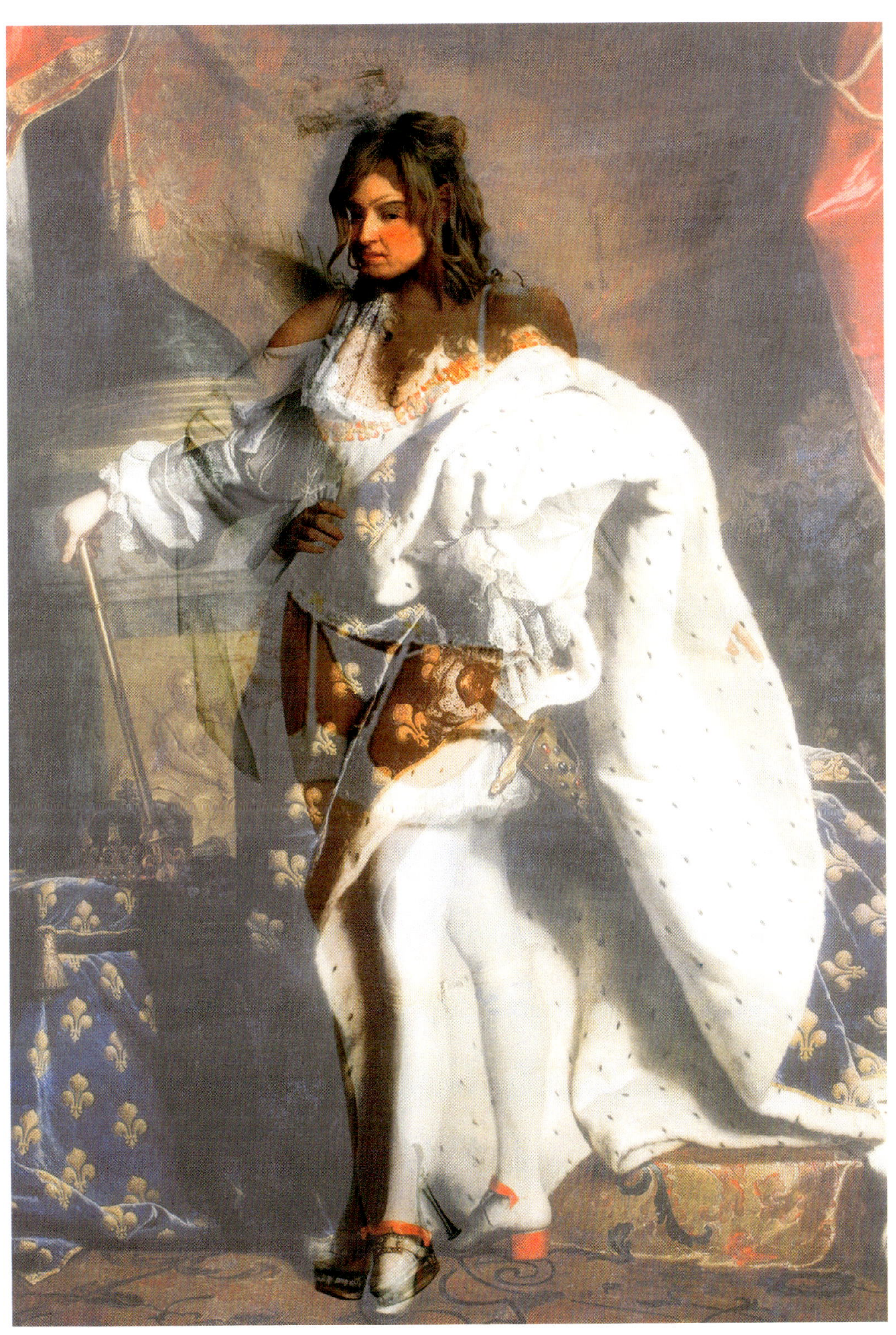

HENK PANDER

(b. 1937, Haarlem, Netherlands; currently lives in Portland, OR)

Last Song, 2010

Oil on linen, 54 ¾ x 65 inches

PROVENANCE

Laura Russo Gallery, Portland, OR (2010)

Collection of Arlene and Harold Schnitzer (December 7, 2010–)

EXHIBITION HISTORY

Henk Pander: New Work, Laura Russo Gallery, Portland Oregon (November 4–27, 2010)

Henk Pander moved from his native Netherlands to Portland in 1965, bringing with him drawing and painting skills fine-tuned at Amsterdam's Rijksacademie. Though at the time Pander planned on an eventual return to his home country, he never moved back, choosing to stay in Portland following his separation from his first wife, Marcia, to be near his sons. Despite having lived in the region for nearly five decades, Pander still considers himself a foreigner, looking at the Northwest experience with an intruder's eye. Pander's thoughtful representations of this reality (sometimes serene, sometime grotesque, and frequently a combination of the two) play with the viewer's sense of memory and interpretation of current events. Keenly aware of the political and social climates and well-versed in traditional art history, he is a master of large-scale, meticulously detailed paintings that address issues of oppression, militarism, absurdity, and loss.

In Pander's large interior painting *Last Song*, the artist pays a moving tribute to his late wife, Delores, whose empty chair is shown in the back of the room behind a table on which a careful arrangement of flowers, a mirror, a book, and a violin sit. These still life elements, several of which extend beyond the edges of the tabletop, directly reference the *vanitas* tradition from seventeenth-century Dutch painting that reminded viewers of the fleetingness of life and emptiness of worldly goods. Pander is one of many artists whose choice to stay in the Northwest, when opportunities to make a living elsewhere existed, has been a defining element throughout their artwork. Schnitzer (who sat for her own portrait by Pander in 1986) has always been perceptive of this phenomenon, and credits the quality of life for artists in the Northwest as a major lure: "You're able to provide for your children. You're able to have medical care. You're able to have a lifestyle that you just don't have in the rooftop lifestyles of New York and Los Angeles."[1]

1 Interview with Schnitzer, September 15, 2011.

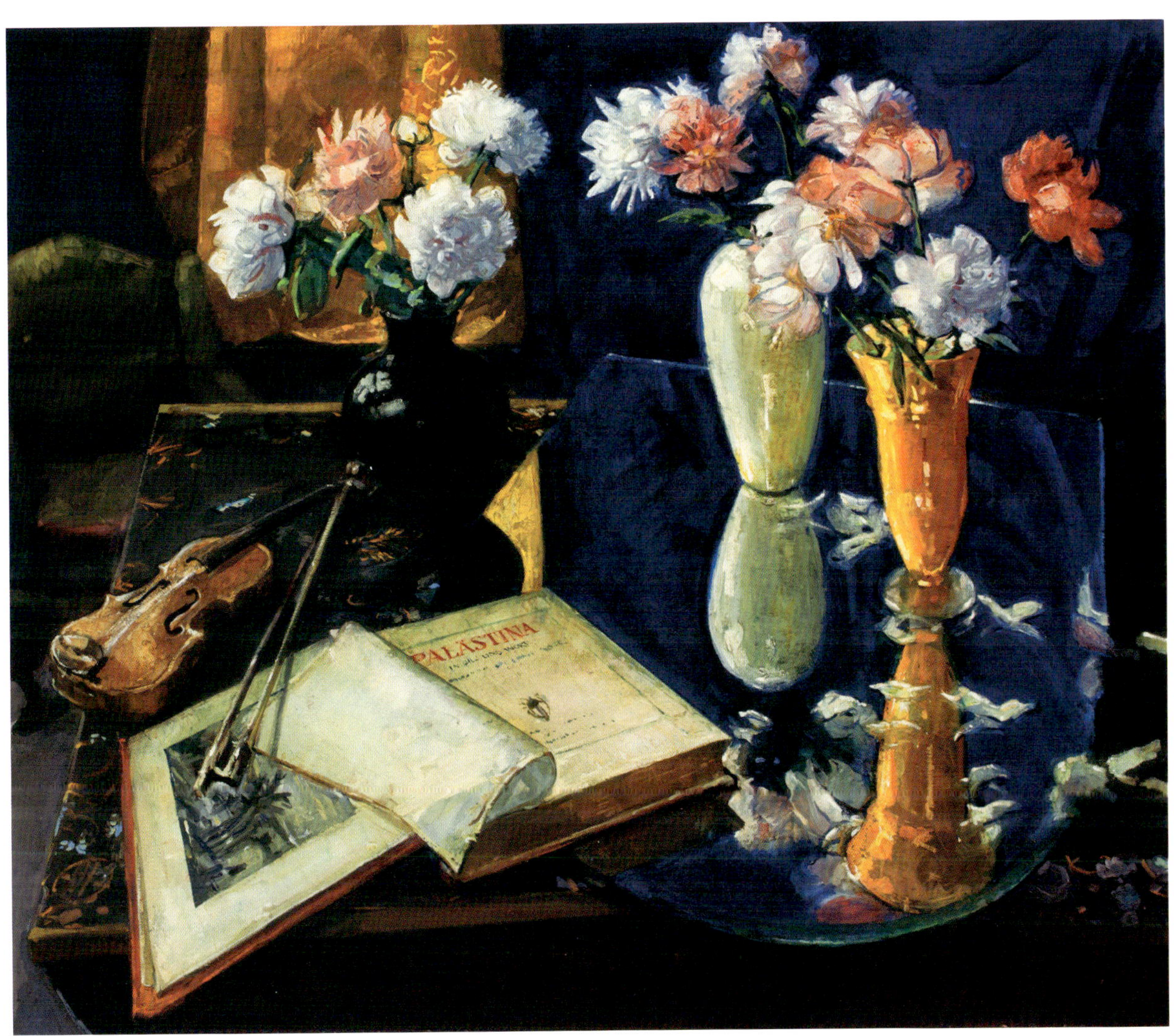
PALÄSTINA

LUCINDA PARKER

(b. 1942, Boston; currently lives in Portland, OR)

Rumpus Jump, 1982

Acrylic on canvas, 61 x 61 inches

PROVENANCE

The Fountain Gallery of Art, Portland, OR (1983)

Collection of Arlene and Harold Schnitzer (March 28, 1983–)

EXHIBITION HISTORY

Lucinda Parker Paintings 1974–1994, Portland Art Museum, OR (September 8–October 22, 1995)

Lucinda Parker creates environments of effusive energy and motion. Born in 1942 in Boston, Parker received a dual BA in painting from Reed College and the Museum Art School (1966) and continued her education with an MFA from the Pratt Institute in New York (1968). Over the years, she has combined Cubism and Abstract Expressionism in her work, paying homage to the legacies of Russian expressionist Wasily Kandinsky and American abstractionists Marsden Hartley and Elizabeth Murray. Her works involve both free gesture and calculated geometry, revealing intricately layered shapes and colors that emerge from deliberation and improvisation. Parker's paintings are vigorously modernist in their formal qualities: each not only emphasizes her physical presence—she enjoys the "smeared" evidence of a maker—but also reinforces the materiality of the paint itself through abstract, non-representational forms. Since her career survey at the Portland Art Museum in 1995, Parker's work has resembled that of C. S. Price, becoming more representational and evocative of the Northwest and its landscape. Like Price, who was born in Iowa, Parker lived and worked elsewhere before discovering the natural majesty of the Northwest. She believes in painting as a form of conveyance: that is, as a conduit that takes the viewer to another place by way of pure vision.

Parker's *Rumpus Jump* from 1982 sends the viewer into a four-squared matrix of spiraling and swirling lines punctuated by bold shapes and colors. She has taken each square and constructed a nearly mirror image on the diagonal, so that the lines and shapes of the squares converge upon a central point. In this way, Parker not only plunges the viewer into the whirling depths of each section, but also lures the viewer into the center of the painting—a potential "vanishing" point of the image that rests paradoxically on the surface of the canvas. According to Schnitzer, who represented Parker at the Fountain Gallery, "When I think of her career, I think of how she told me how much she has been influenced by Price. I am very conscious of relationships when I install work. I have a painting by Lucinda in my bedroom and one by Price in my living room. You can see the relationship between them."[1]

1 Quoted in "Lucinda Parker, A Symphony of Shapes." D.K. Row, *The Oregonian*, Saturday, January 5, 2008, http://blog.oregonlive.com/visualarts/2008/01/lucinda_parker_a_symphony_of_s.html. Accessed March 6, 2012.

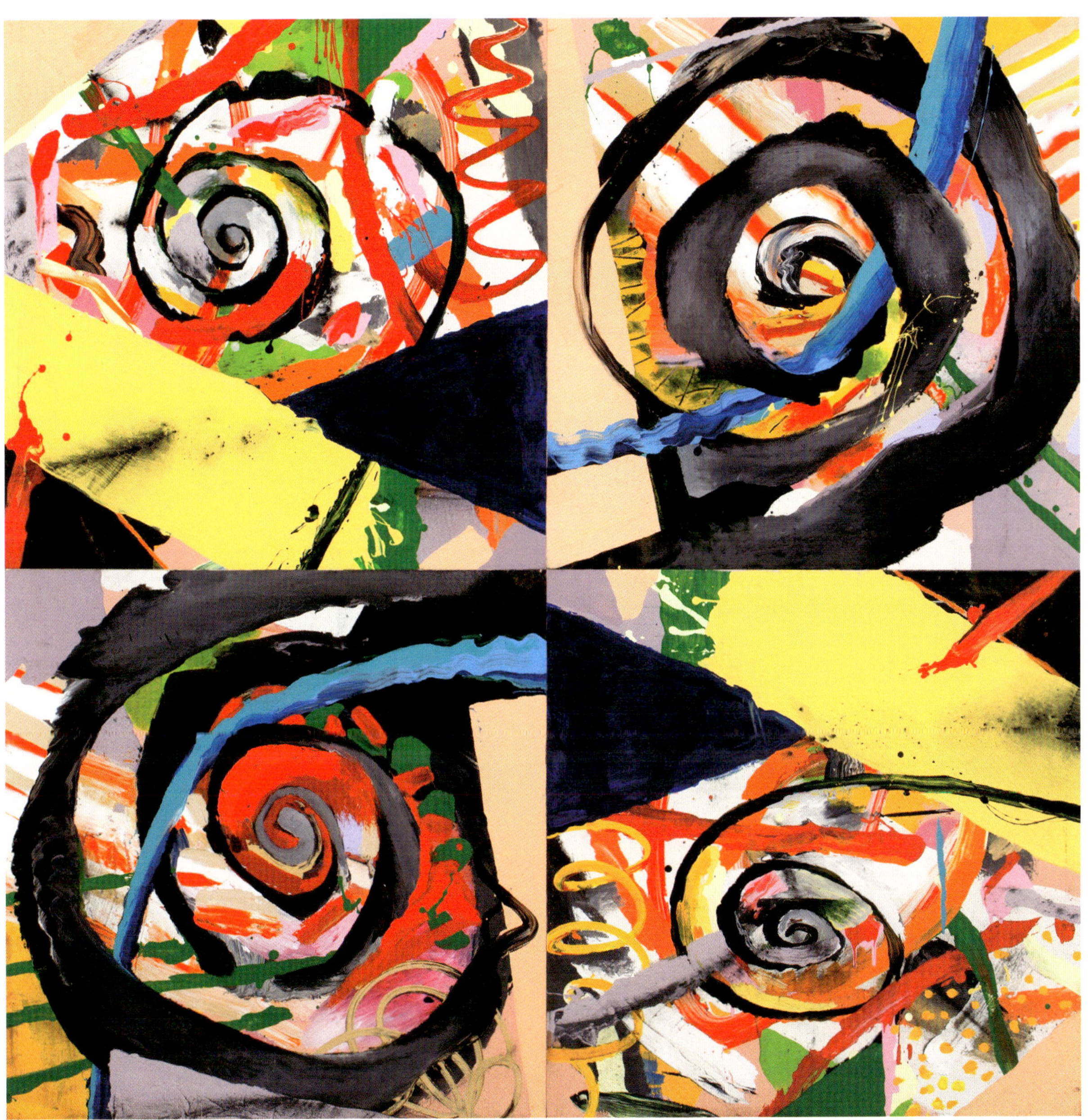

JACK PORTLAND

(b. 1946, San Luis Obispo, CA; currently lives in Portland, OR, and Rome, Italy)

Senso Unico, 1991

Oil on canvas, 53 ½ x 47 inches

PROVENANCE

Laura Russo Gallery, Portland, OR (1991)

Collection of Arlene and Harold Schnitzer (September 4, 1991-)

EXHIBITION HISTORY

Solo Show, Laura Russo Gallery, Portland, OR (1991)

Born in San Luis Obispo, CA, Jack Portland relocated to Oregon in the 1960s. With a burgeoning interest in drawing and watercolor, he enrolled at the Museum Art School in 1971, where Louis Bunce and Michele Russo, among others, served as his mentors. He then began a career in Portland as an artist and teacher. After his children left the family nest, Portland traveled to Rome to pursue his lifelong interest in fresco painting; he now spends half the year in Oregon, completing smaller oils and watercolors, and the other half in Italy painting frescoes. His work has been shown nationally and internationally and is held in several private and public collections across the country. His public commissions are displayed currently throughout Portland: in the Portland International Airport, the St. Philip Neri Parish, the Southeast Portland Police Precinct, and Western Oregon University. The intricately woven paintings of Portland's early work gave way after 1993—when he began to divide his time between Italy and the Northwest—to looser compositions that combined landscapes and still lifes with his former vibrant color palette and abstracted forms.

Portland utilizes elements of Impressionism, Expressionism, and Surrealism to craft fantastical landscapes, still lifes, and abstract forms. In his earlier paintings, including *Senso Unico,* Portland fashioned phantasmagorical scenes through the interplay of abstract and geometrical shapes that he varied according to pattern, color, and texture. His work was exhibited in many shows at the Fountain Gallery, and he had an especially close friendship with Bunce ("Nobody could be any more of a son to anybody, than Jack was to Louis," recalled Schnitzer[1]). In 1985, Schnitzer recounted an incident in which Portland told her, "I've hired you; this is what the gallery relationship really is. You work for the artists. Any time I don't like the relationship, I can get up and walk out."[2] Schnitzer replied, "And that's really true."[3]

1 Interview with Schnitzer, September 15, 2011.

2 *Oral history interview with Arlene Schnitzer, conducted by Bruce Guenther, June 7–8, 1985. Archives of American Art, Smithsonian Institution.*

3 Interview with Schnitzer, September 15, 2011.

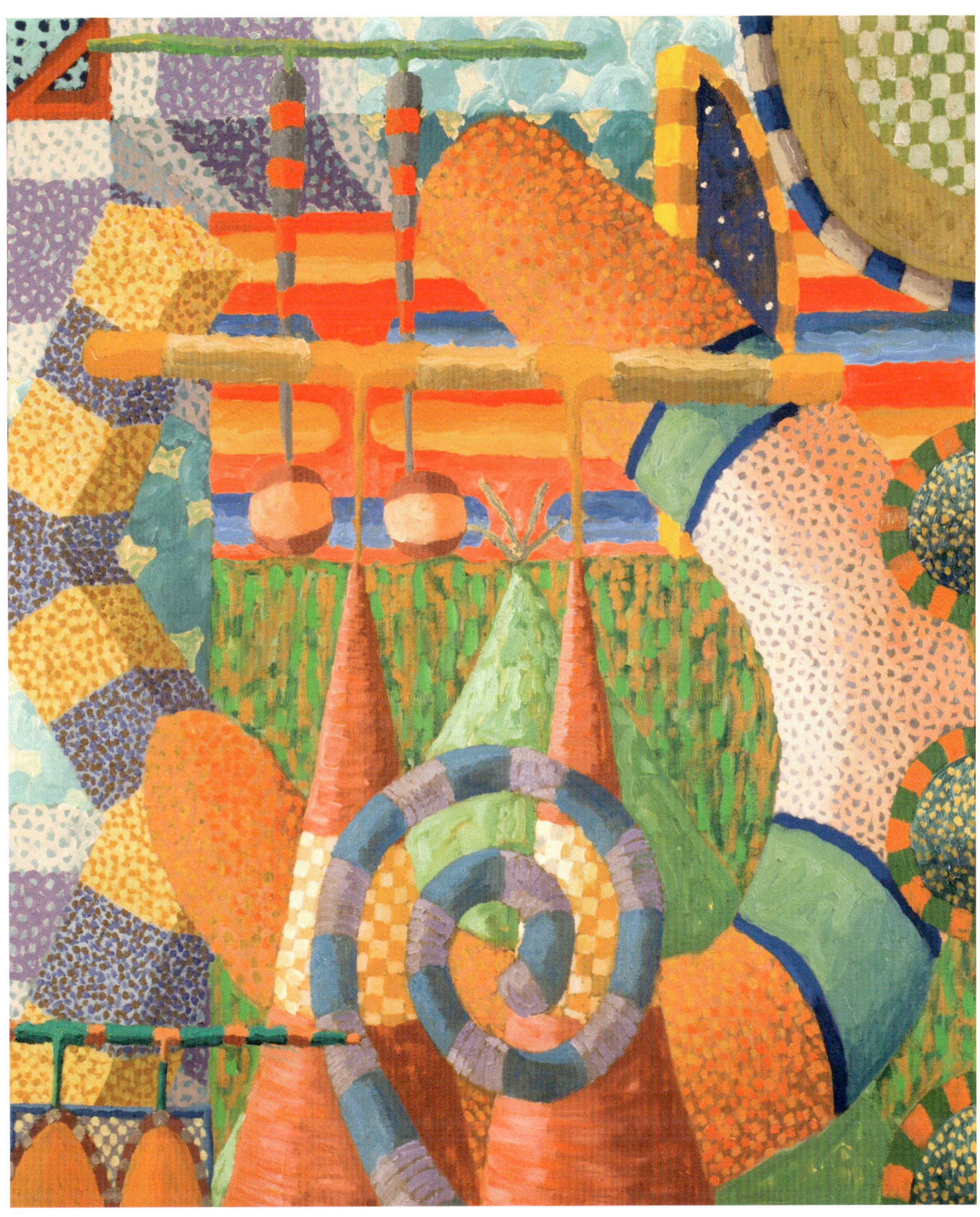

C.S. PRICE

(b. 1874, Bedford, IA; d. 1950, Portland, OR)

***By the River*, 1927**

Oil on board, 30 ½ x 37 inches

PROVENANCE

Collection of Mrs. J. M. Roby (by 1942)

Collection of Frank Webb

The Fountain Gallery of Art, Portland, OR (1967)

Collection of Arlene and Harold Schnitzer (1967–)

EXHIBITION HISTORY

Monterey Art Festival, CA (1927)

C.S. Price Retrospective Exhibition of Paintings 1920–1942, Portland Art Museum, OR (February 1942)

A Tribute to C.S. Price, Portland Art Museum, OR (September 14–October 17, 1976)

Collective Visions: Six Local Collections, Portland Center for the Visual Arts, Portland, OR (May 3–June 2, 1984)

Portland Collects, Portland Art Museum, OR (March 4–May 2, 1993)

California Progressives 1910–1930, Laguna Art Museum, CA (October 26, 1996– January 12, 1997)

C.S. Price: Landscape, Image, and Spirit, Saint Mary's College of California Hearst Art Gallery, Moraga, CA; also traveled to Jordan Schnitzer Museum of Art, Eugene, OR; Monterey Museum of Art, CA (June 1998–April 1999).

Born in rural Iowa, Clayton Sumner Price was raised in a ranching culture and had an early introduction to the physical and emotional toil of working the land. These firsthand experiences were formative for his developing artistic sensibilities. As a young man he carried a sketchbook with him, while tending to the family's livestock, to record his experiences. Price's only formal artistic training came in 1905, when he enrolled for a year's study at the St. Louis Museum School of Fine Arts. In 1909, the aspiring artist found work in Portland illustrating *Pacific Monthly Magazine*. Over the next two decades, he relocated frequently, painting the western experience from British Columbia to California. After participating in the artists' colony in Monterey during the 1920s, Price returned to Portland, where he was hired as a WPA artist. By that time, he had moved beyond his early literal mode of representation in the tradition of cowboy artists like his friend Charles M. Russell; seeing the work of Paul Cézanne and the European modernists had caused a revelation in Price's art-making, and he began to use color in a profoundly emotional and responsive way. His later, loosely painted works celebrated the essential qualities of his subject matter. Price spent the rest of his life in Oregon and was honored with a retrospective at the Portland Art Museum in 1942, inclusion in the Museum of Modern Art's exhibition *Fourteen Americans* in 1946, and a memorial exhibition at the Portland Art Museum in 1951. He has been of great influence to such Northwest artists as Charles Heaney and the Runquist brothers, Albert and Arthur.

Schnitzer's first experience seeing the work of Price was extremely positive. At the time, Schnitzer had just started her classes at the Museum Art School and Price's 1937 WPA oil on canvas mural *Huckleberry Pickers* (now installed in the C.S. Price Wing at Timberline Lodge, Mount Hood, OR) was on view in the museum. She had an immediate response to it, fondly remembering, "The day I walked into art school I saw that. [It] really stands out in my memories."[1] Over the decades the Schnitzers acquired examples of his work from several different periods for their own collection.[2] Though she never had the opportunity to meet him, Schnitzer is mindful of how large Price's legacy looms over the Northwest artists

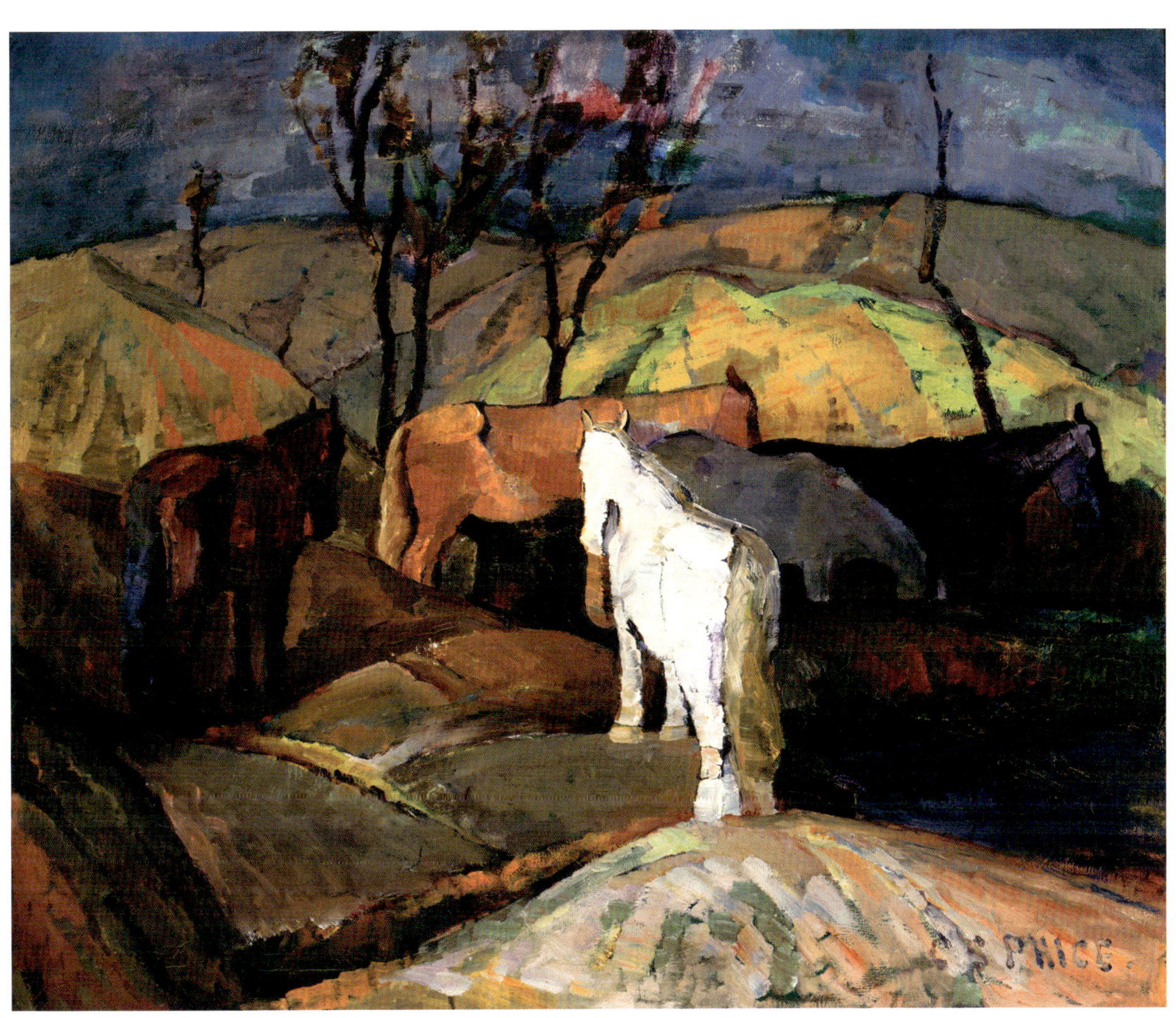
PRICE.

C.S. PRICE

Cattle by the River, 1940

Oil on canvas, 30 x 34 inches

PROVENANCE

Collection of Dr. Harry Austin Blutman (by 1946)

James Goodman Gallery, New York, NY

Pensler Galleries, Washington, DC (early 1990s–1998)

Collection of Arlene and Harold Schnitzer (February 11, 1998–)

EXHIBITIONS

Fourteen Americans, Museum of Modern Art, New York, NY (1946)

C.S. Price 1874–1950—A Memorial Exhibition, Portland Art Museum, OR (March 8–April 18, 1951); also traveled to Seattle Art Museum, WA; Los Angeles County Museum, CA; Baltimore Museum of Art, MD; Munson-William-Proctor Institute, Utica, NY; Detroit Institute of Arts, MI; Walker Art Center, Minneapolis, MN; California Palace of the Legion of Honor, San Francisco; and Santa Barbara Museum of Art, CA.

C.S. Price, The Downtown Gallery, New York, NY (January 28–February 21, 1958)

C.S. Price: Landscape, Image, and Spirit, Saint Mary's College of California Hearst Art Gallery, Moraga, CA; also traveled to Jordan Schnitzer Museum of Art, Eugene, OR; Monterey Museum of Art, CA (June 1998–April 1999).

who followed—and for Schnitzer, who has always valued deep relationships, this ability for his artwork to resonate so strongly with other visual artists makes his work even more compelling.

By the River (1927) and *Cattle by the River* (1940), two large oil paintings in the Arlene and Harold Schnitzer art collection, illustrate the changes in Price's philosophy of art-making that occurred as his early Monterey style fell away, and he became increasingly invested in using his art to record emotional and spiritual responses to his surroundings. *Cattle by the River*'s bold forms fill the composition; the background, rather than depicting an easily identifiable landscape, consists of broad stripes of color that give the impression of the horizon.

Five handcarved animal forms (page 20), each only a few inches in height, provide insight into Price's method of visual engagement with his subjects. These small horses and cows, which he whittled in 1937, were used by the artist to set up tableaus for his many drawing and painting projects. By examining these three-dimensional animals, he could think more holistically about how to translate their physical forms into two-dimensional paint.

A suite of small oil paintings (page 74) that range in date from 1915 to 1948 capture many of Price's favorite recurring subjects: livestock, the land, and the sea. A set of four drawings (page 75) made by lithographic crayon on paper, which date from late in Price's life, show scenes reminiscent of his earlier time on the California coast, though stylistically they are evident of the work that he did while living in Oregon. Schnitzer explained the process by which Price made these images, by drawing thickly with the grease crayon and then scraping back through his marks with a razor blade.[3]

1 Interview with Schnitzer, September 15, 2011.

2 Many of these came to Schnitzer by way of her friend James Van Evera Bailey and his wife. While living in California during the Great Depression, Van Bailey (professionally, he shortened his name) had collaborated with architect William Grey Purcell, under whom he had studied in Portland years prior, and both men knew Price personally. The couple would often stop by the Fountain Gallery to show Schnitzer works by Price in which they thought she'd have an interest.

3 Interview with Schnitzer, November 7, 2011.

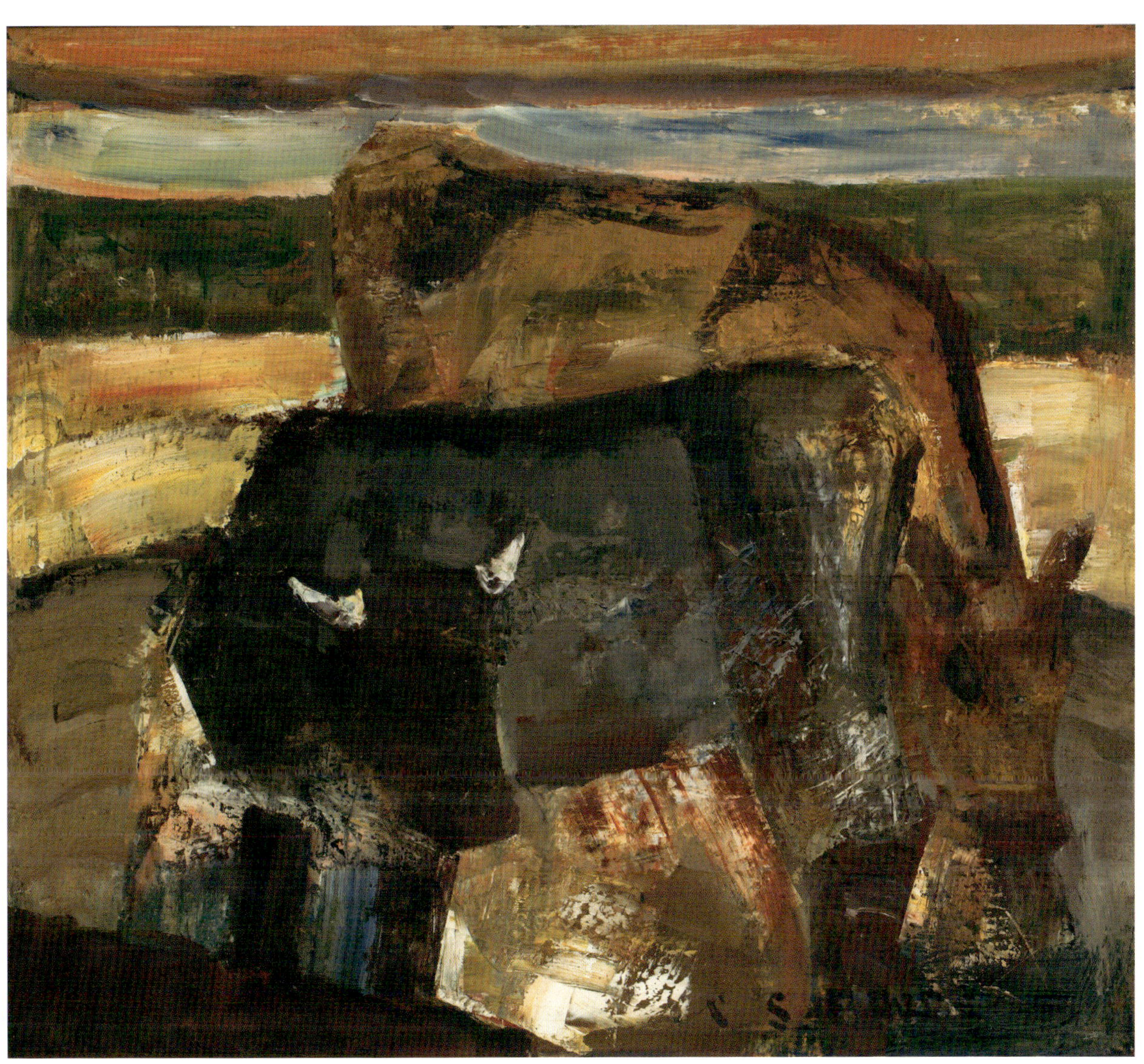

C.S. PRICE

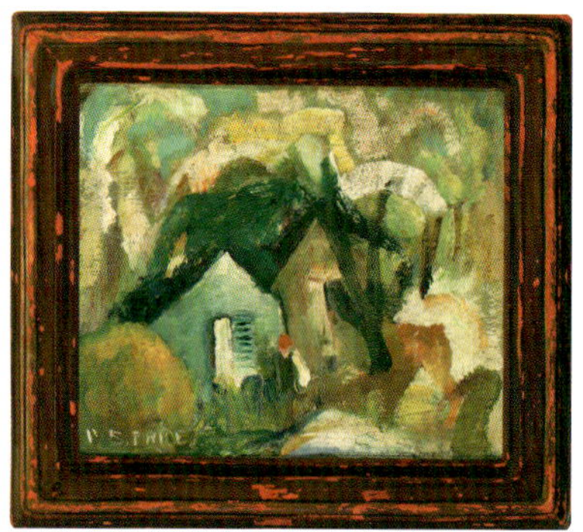

Man and Houses, c. 1926–28
Oil on masonite, 9 ¾ x 11 ½ inches

PROVENANCE
Collection of William Gray Purcell
Collection of Mr. and Mrs. James Van Evera Bailey
Collection of Arlene and Harold Schnitzer (November 15, 1971–)

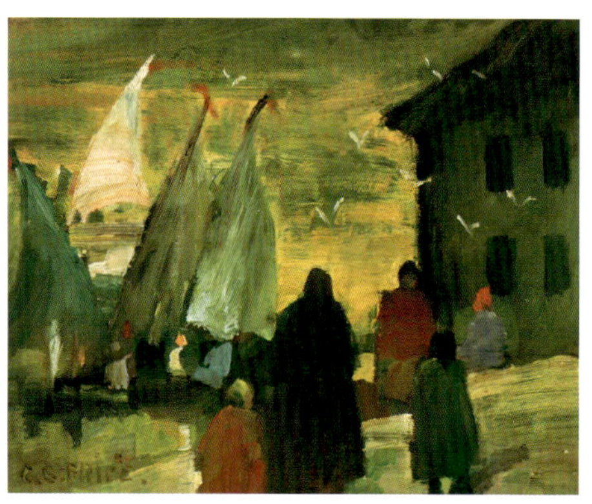

Untitled (Figures and Boats), c. 1948
Oil on board, 13 x 16 inches

PROVENANCE
Pioneer Antique Auction, Portland, OR
Collection of Arlene and Harold Schnitzer (March 24, 1996–)

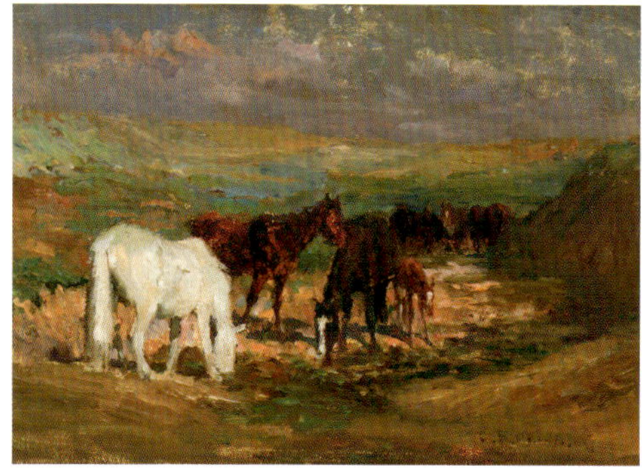

Eight Horses, 1915
Oil on canvas, 8 x 11 ¾ inches

PROVENANCE
Collection of William and Violet Dominick
Collection of Arlene and Harold Schnitzer (March 18, 1970–)

EXHIBITION HISTORY
A Tribute to C.S. Price, Portland Art Museum, OR
(September 14–October 17, 1976)

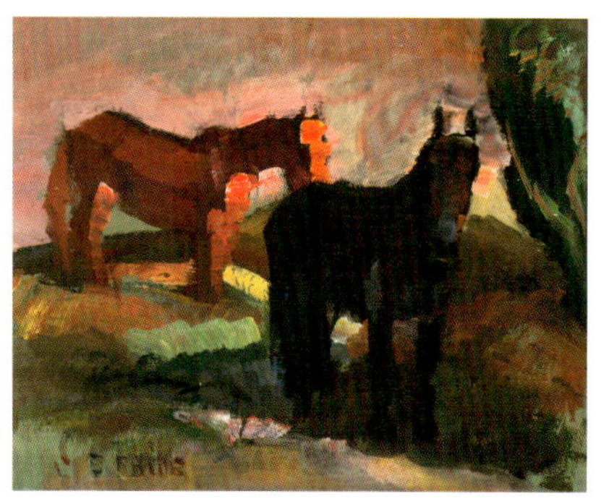

Untitled (Horses in Landscape), n.d.
Oil on board, 12 x 15 inches

PROVENANCE
Argus Gallery
Collection of Arlene and Harold Schnitzer (November 15, 1989–)

The Ferry, late 1940s
Lithographic crayon on paper, 3 x 4 inches

PROVENANCE
Collection of William Gray Purcell
Collection of Mr. and Mrs. James Van Evera Bailey
Collection of Arlene and Harold Schnitzer (November 25, 1971–)

EXHIBITION HISTORY
A Tribute to C.S. Price, Portland Art Museum, OR
(September 14–October 17, 1976)

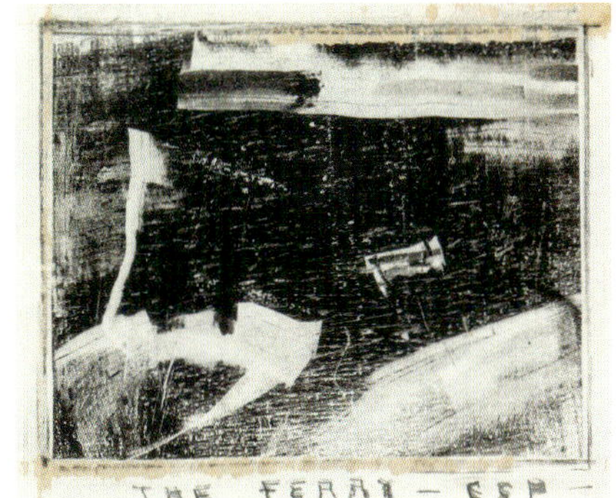

Waterfront Scene, late 1940s
Lithographic crayon on paper, 3 ¼ x 4 ¾ inches

PROVENANCE
Collection of William Gray Purcell
Collection of Mr. and Mrs. James Van Evera Bailey
Collection of Arlene and Harold Schnitzer (November 25, 1971–)

EXHIBITION HISTORY
A Tribute to C.S. Price, Portland Art Museum, OR
September 14–October 17, 1976)

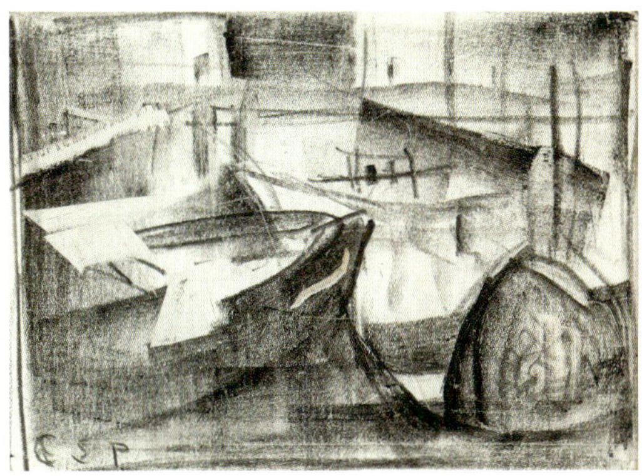

Untitled (dark landscape with buildings), late 1940s
Lithographic crayon on paper, 3 ¼ x 4 ¾ inches

PROVENANCE
Collection of William Gray Purcell
Collection of Mr. and Mrs. James Van Evera Bailey
Collection of Arlene and Harold Schnitzer (November 25, 1971–)

EXHIBITION HISTORY
A Tribute to C.S. Price, Portland Art Museum, OR
(September 14–October 17, 1976)

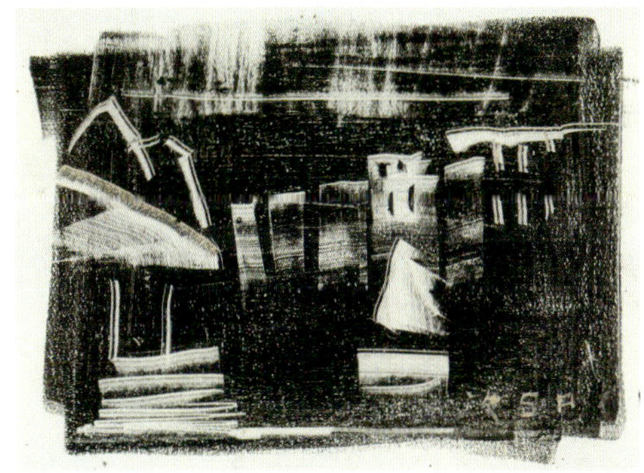

Untitled (landscape with houses), late 1940s
Lithographic crayon on paper, 3 ½ x 5 ¾ inches

PROVENANCE
Collection of William Gray Purcell
Collection of Mr. and Mrs. James Van Evera Bailey
Collection of Arlene and Harold Schnitzer (November 25, 1971–)

EXHIBITION HISTORY
A Tribute to C.S. Price, Portland Art Museum, OR
(September 14–October 17, 1976)

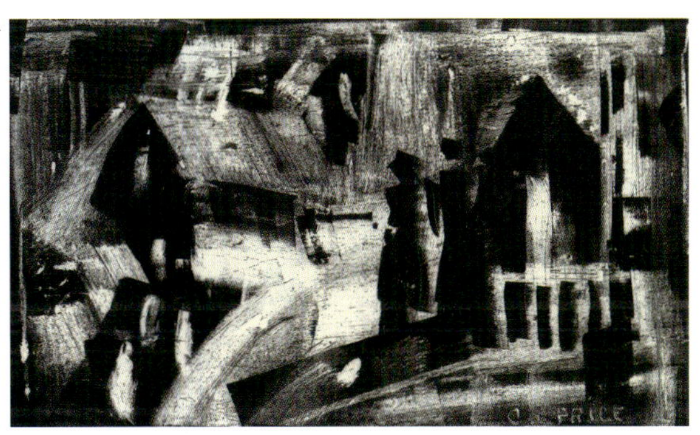

RENÉ RICKABAUGH

(b. 1947, Portland, OR; currently lives in Portland, OR)

Manchild, 1990

Ceramic, 12½ x 8 x 9 inches

PROVENANCE

Laura Russo Gallery, Portland, OR (1990)

Collection of Arlene and Harold Schnitzer (January 15, 1990–)

EXHIBITION HISTORY

Solo exhibition, Laura Russo Gallery, Portland, OR (1990)

Spider Bite, 1983

Watercolor on paper, 11 x 11 ½ inches

PROVENANCE

The Fountain Gallery of Art, Portland, OR (1983)

Collection of Arlene and Harold Schnitzer (February 3, 1983–)

René Rickabaugh was born in Portland in 1947 to an artistic family, and he attended the Museum Art School, from which he graduated with a BFA in 1970. Rickabaugh has achieved wide recognition for his watercolors in which he depicts a variety of natural subjects with miniaturist detail. His is a highly decorative art, evocative of pre-Columbian, Middle Eastern, and East Indian aesthetics, and his imagery often includes birds, plants, and floral themes. He has shown prolifically in Portland, at the Laura Russo Gallery, the Froelick Gallery (2008), the Fountain Gallery (1977, 1981, 1983, 1985), and outside the state, at the Gail Severn Gallery in Ketchum, Idaho (1993, 2007, 2009), the Traver/Sutton Gallery in Seattle (1986, 1987), and the Allan Stone Gallery in New York City (1982). His work has also been featured in solo exhibitions at the Portland Art Museum (1981) and the Jordan Schnitzer Museum of Art at the University of Oregon (1980).

Schnitzer remarked on Rickabaugh's capacity, evident in *Manchild,* to evoke the visual effect of bronze and patina while working in ceramics. Rickabaugh accentuates a brown base hue with subtle tinges of green, dispersed across the statue's surface. He lends an importance to the figure by means of its upright seated posture, resembling the imagery of royal portraits, an architectonic solidity, and a contemplative facial expression. "I think this is a portrait of himself, as a boy," said Schnitzer, who especially delights in the artist's inclusion of a small frog on the subject's wrist. "It's wonderful. I treasure this. I really do."[1]

In *Spider Bite,* Rickabaugh displays a dual interest in decorative ornament and human expression. A lone child stands in an expansive field, surrounded by flowers that the artist has meticulously differentiated and colored. Rickabaugh's title alone provides evidence to the cause of the boy's apparent discomfort. The composition bears a notable balance and symmetry that serves to eternalize and generalize this moment.

1 Interview with Schnitzer, September 15, 2011.

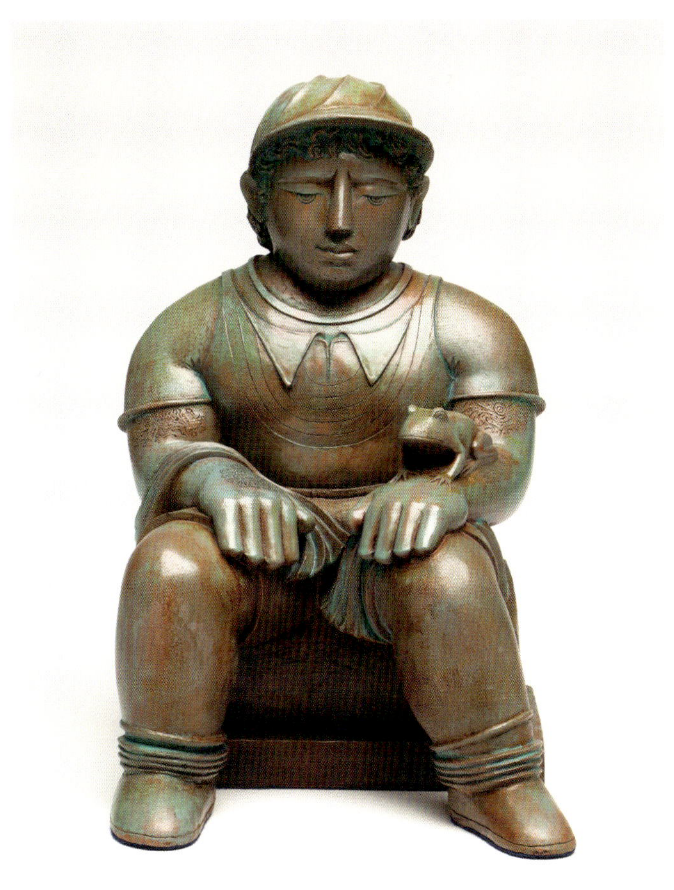

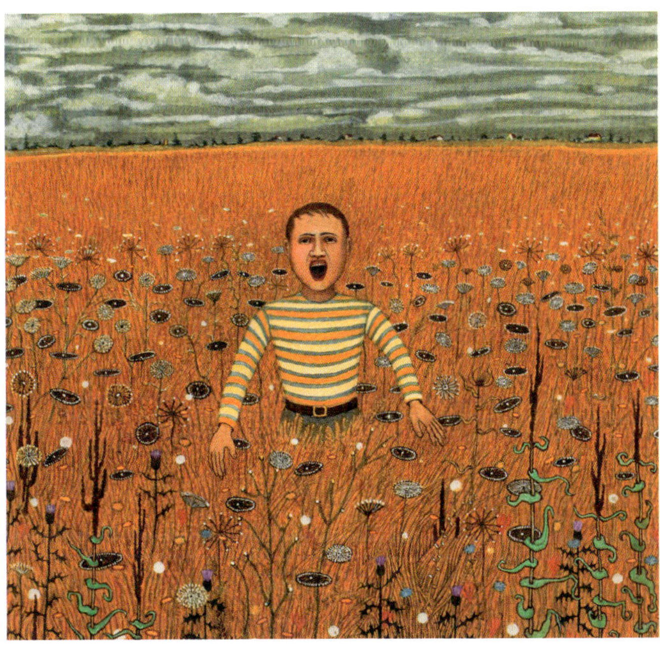

MICHELE RUSSO

(b. 1909, Waterbury, CT; d. 2004, Portland, OR)

Girl with Daisies, c. 1950

Oil on burlap, 56 x 46 inches

PROVENANCE

The Fountain Gallery of Art, Portland, OR (1962)

Heathman Hotel, Portland, OR (June 29, 1962–1982)

Collection of Arlene and Harold Schnitzer (1982–)

EXHIBITION HISTORY

Michele Russo, A Fifty Year Retrospective, Oregon Art Institute, Portland Art Museum, OR (August 12–October 9, 1988)

The Life and Art of Michele Russo, Pacific Northwest College of Art, Portland, OR (March 3–April 30, 2005)

Michele "Mike" Russo was born to Italian immigrants and spent much of his childhood living in Italy, when the family was unable to return to the U.S. following a visit during World War I. After graduating with a BFA from Yale University in 1934, he married artist Sally Haley the following year and took additional coursework at the Colorado Springs Fine Arts Center (1937). As a WPA artist, he completed murals in Hamden and New Haven, Connecticut. In 1947, the couple moved to Portland, where Russo began teaching art history at the Museum Art School, a position he would hold for twenty-seven years. It was Russo who taught the very first course Schnitzer took as a new enrollee in 1958, and his nuanced understanding of art history made a tremendous impression on her long before she ever saw one of his own paintings. Russo cofounded the Portland Center for the Visual Arts with Mel Katz and Jay Backstrand in 1972. For fifteen years, the PCVA was a major force in shaping the city's contemporary art scene. While teaching and running the PCVA, Russo also poured his energy into advocating for artists (he helped institute Oregon's One Percent for Public Art program in 1975 and also pushed tirelessly for legislation protecting artists' rights in the state). At the time of his passing at age 95 in 2004, Russo was considered one of Oregon's more important modernists and had secured his legacy as not just a talented artist, but also an influential teacher and inspiring community leader.

Schnitzer represented Russo at the Fountain Gallery from the very beginning; his work was included in her first show, *Opening Exhibition*, alongside fourteen other artists from the Northwest, California, Colorado, and Illinois. Though Russo's work was initially difficult to sell due to its unconventional style and controversial subject matter—his paintings were a strong departure from the traditional figurative artwork with which most of Portland's citizenry were more familiar—Schnitzer remained steadfast in her belief that his talent and genius were vital to Portland's growing modern art community. In a 2003 interview, she called him "a great example of persevering, of following his own vision . . . he's a star."[1] *Girl with Daisies* was the Fountain Gallery's first corporate sale, made to the Heathman Hotel in the early 1960s, where it was hung above the bar and caused some public outrage over its perceived indecency. Years later, when the hotel was being renovated, Schnitzer purchased it back for her private collection.

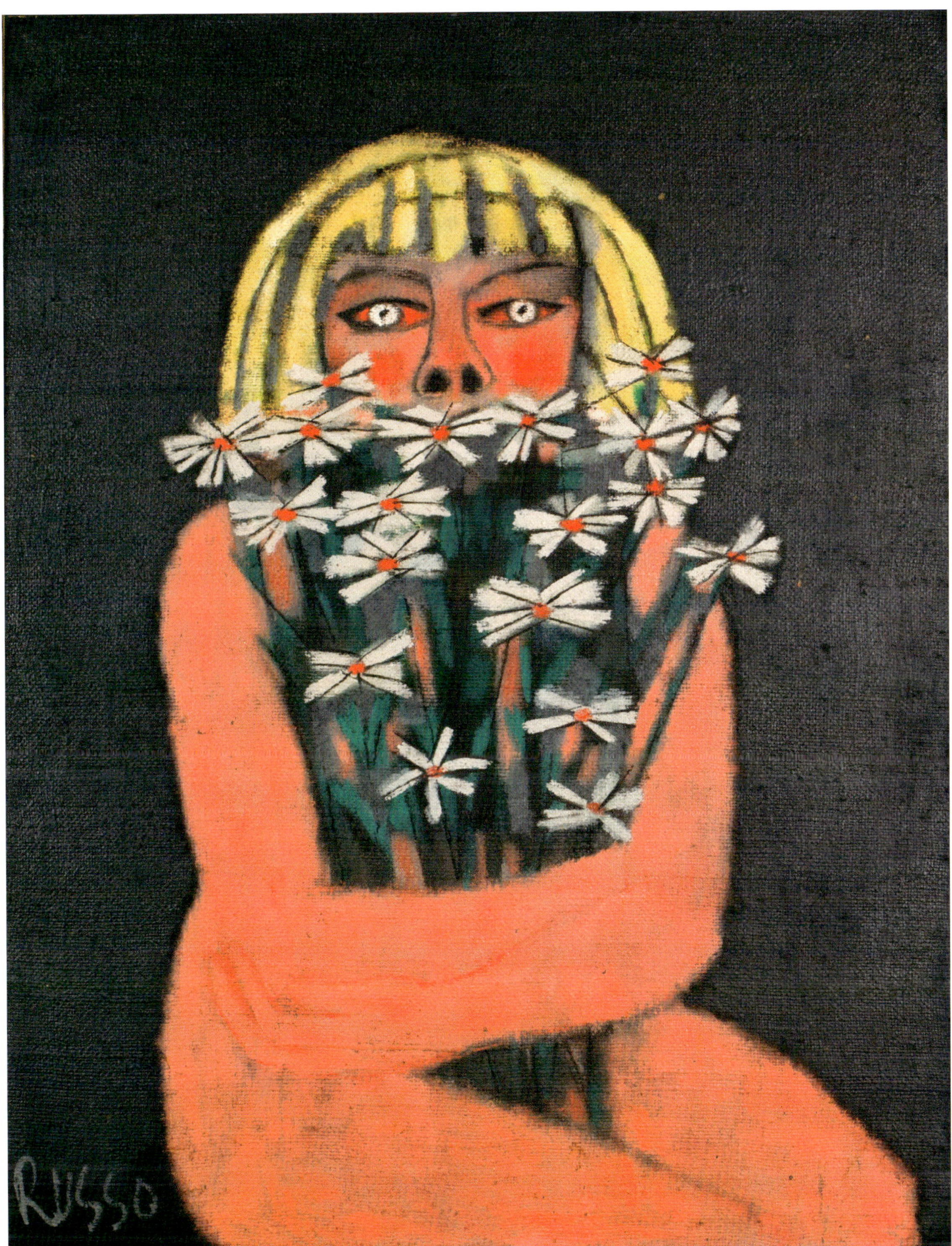
RUSSO

MICHELE RUSSO

To Move, To Breathe, To Speak, 1960

Oil on burlap, 62 x 49 inches

PROVENANCE

Collection of Arlene and Harold Schnitzer (c. 1961–)

EXHIBITION HISTORY

Michele Russo, Paintings 1956–1966, Portland Art Museum, OR (October 30–November 27, 1966)

Art of the Pacific Northwest: from the 1930s to the Present, Smithsonian Institution National Collection of Fine Arts, Washington, DC (February 8–May 5, 1974)

Michele Russo, A Fifty Year Retrospective, Oregon Art Institute, Portland Art Museum, OR (August 12–October 9, 1988)

Jet Dreams, Art of the Fifties, Tacoma Art Museum, WA (March 16–June 4, 1995)

The Life and Art of Michele Russo, Pacific Northwest College of Art, Portland, OR (March 3–April 30, 2005)

PNCA at 100, Portland Art Museum, OR (June 6–September 13, 2009)

Portland Collects: Riches of a City, Portland Art Museum, OR (February 5–May 22, 2011)

In describing Russo's work, Schnitzer reflected on what she called "so typical" for the artist: "exactly what Mike was aiming for—the androgynous, his palette, and true mysticism of the human figure. . . . And sexuality, absolute sexuality."[2] *To Move, To Breathe, To Speak* is one of his most accomplished paintings and is of even greater personal value to Schnitzer; Russo gave it to her as a gift, an act she later called as "one of the most touching moments in my 'art' lifetime."[3] In 1974, the Smithsonian Institution approached Schnitzer and asked to purchase the painting from her. Though Schnitzer did not want to part with it, she decided to leave the decision up to Russo, explaining: ". . . I called Mike. I said, 'Mike, they want to buy this painting, and I'll leave that up to you. . . . I don't want to keep you out of the [Smithsonian] collection, but you know, it's your decision.' He said, 'If you sell that painting to them, all they're going to do is put it in the basement, in storage, and it will just gather dust.' And I said, 'So what are you saying?' And he said, 'I'm saying you keep it.' So I did."[4] Fittingly, Russo, who had been one of Schnitzer's gallery artists from the start, was included in the Fountain Gallery's final exhibition, *Twenty-fifth Anniversary Group Show,* in June 1968.

1 Eric Cane, producer. *Oregon Art Beat: Painter Mike Russo*. 2003. (http://www.opb.org/programs/artbeat/segments/view/523) Accessed March 13, 2012.

2 Interview with Schnitzer, September 15, 2011.

3 *The Life and Art of Michele Russo* (Portland, OR: Pacific Northwest College of Art, 2005), 9.

4 Interview with Schnitzer, September 15, 2011.

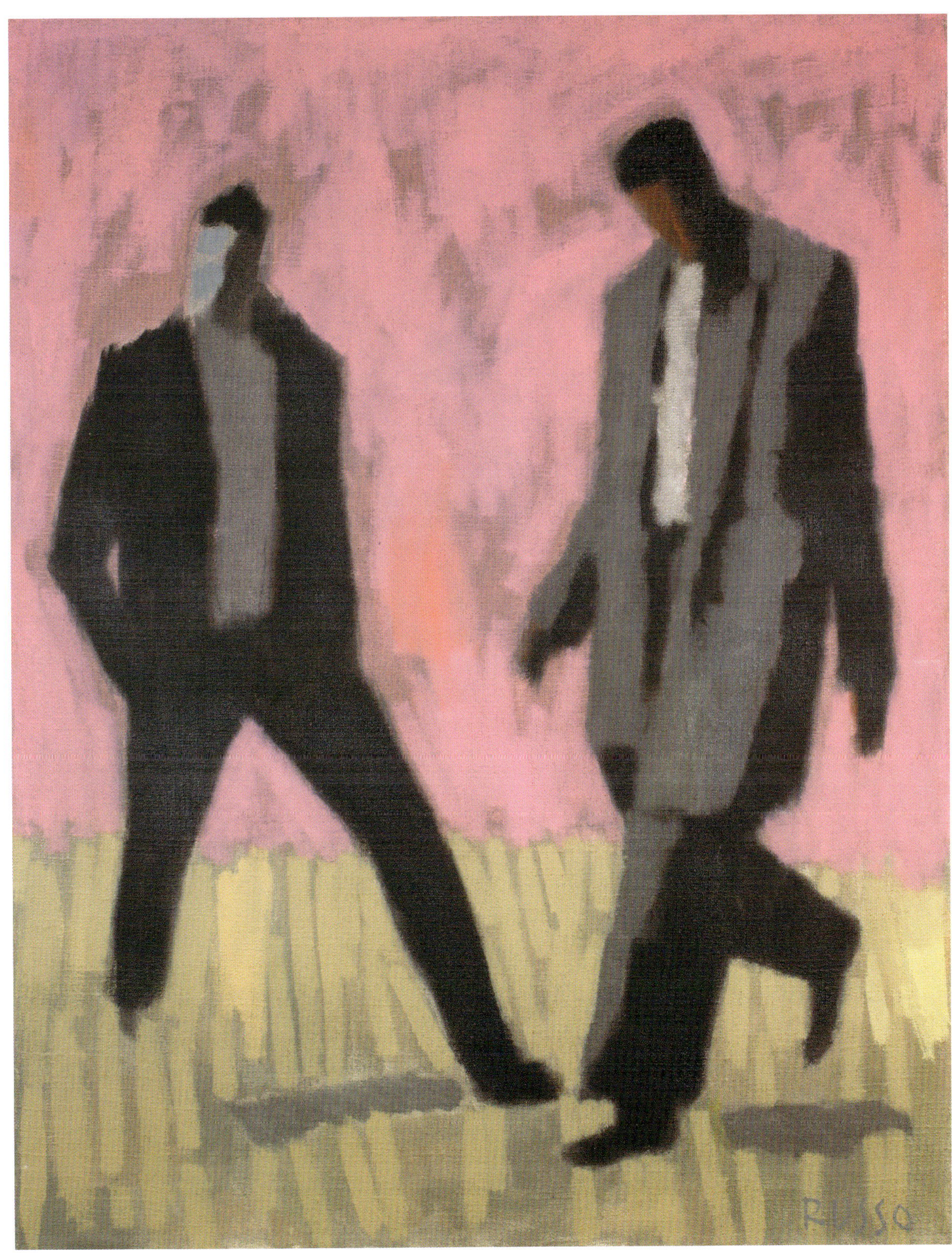
RUSSO

AKIO TAKAMORI

(b. 1950, Nobeoka, Miyazaki, Japan; currently lives in Seattle, WA)

Kanzan, 2006

Stoneware with underglaze, 45 x 22 x 18 inches

Jittoku, 2006

Stoneware with underglaze, 45 x 22 x 18 inches

PROVENANCE

James Harris Gallery, Seattle, WA (2007)

Collection of Arlene and Harold Schnitzer (Sept. 21, 2007–)

EXHIBITION HISTORY

Jupiter Affair, Jupiter Hotel, Portland, OR (2007)

Akio Takamori works primarily in figurative sculpture, and his art frequently carries an autobiographical element. He relies on memories from his childhood in Japan to inspire statues of villagers, children, and shopkeepers. His father was a dermatologist whose extensive library of both art and medical texts fascinated and influenced the young Takamori. Upon graduating from the Musashino Art College at the University of Tokyo, he was apprenticed as a potter in Koshiwara. An influential meeting with American ceramicist Ken Ferguson convinced him to move to the United States, which he did in 1974. Takamori received his BFA from the Kansas City Art Institute (1976) and later his MFA from Alfred University in Alfred, NY (1978). He moved to Seattle in 1993, where he began work in the Ceramics Department at the University of Washington and now holds the title of Professor and Co-chair of the Art Department. Takamori is a three-time recipient of National Endowment for the Arts grants (1986, 1988, 1992) and has also received a Virginia A. Groot Foundation grant (2001), a Flintridge Foundation Award for Visual Artists (2004), a Joan Mitchell Foundation Award (2006), and the Neddy Artist Fellowship for Painting and Ceramics (2008).

Takamori drew from native Japanese imagery to create his large stoneware figures *Kanzan* and *Jittoku*, who bear strong resemblance to one another. The characters of Kanzan and Jittoku originated in Zen Buddhist folklore and have been popular subjects in Japanese and Chinese painting for centuries; known as the "Laughing Monks," they represent the delightful nature of children and the elderly. Takamori, who is interested in mirror-imagery, has created several near-identical representations of these figures in recent years. The historical Kanzan was a mountain recluse and poet and his young friend, Jittoku, was an orphan employed as a dishwasher at a monastery. The sculpted pair's stature, roughly two-thirds life-size, makes for an uncertain interaction between viewer and object. Takamori has given his figures facial expressions full of character and joviality, lending a playfulness to the pair. "I think these are fabulous," Schnitzer has exclaimed of her monks. "Aren't they wonderful?"[1]

1 Interview with Schnitzer, September 15, 2011.

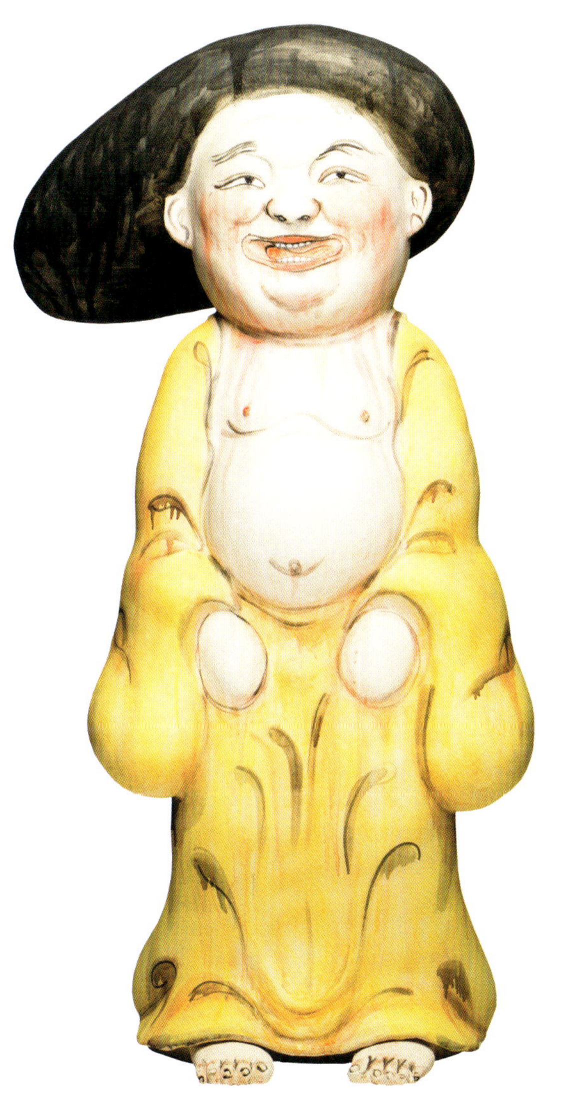

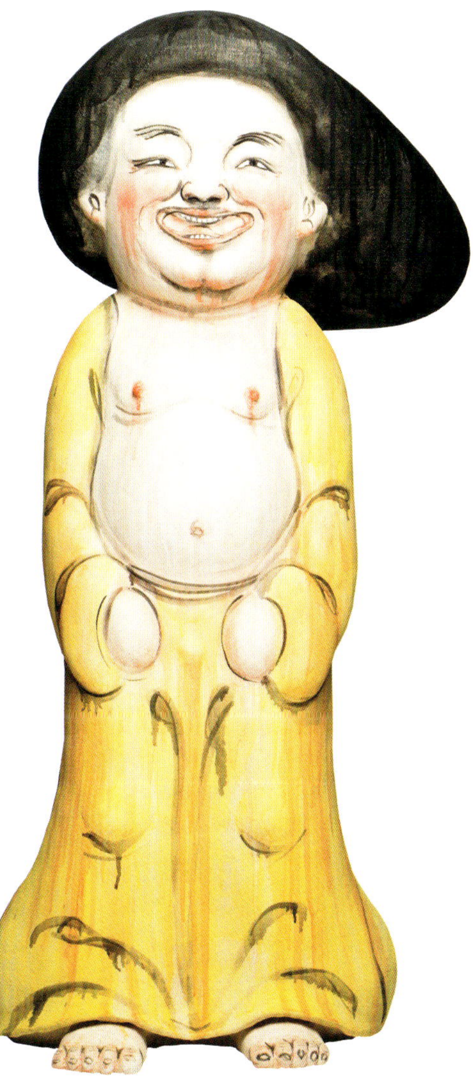

MARK TOBEY

(b. 1890, Centerville, WI; d. 1976, Basel, Switzerland)

Two Market Figures, 1940

Egg tempera on paper, 30 ½ x 24 inches

PROVENANCE

Collection of Donald and Mollie Young

Collection of Arlene and Harold Schnitzer (April 11, 1980–)

Wisconsin-born Mark Tobey was primarily self-taught; brief studies at the Art Institute of Chicago in the late 1910s were followed by several freelance art and design jobs in other cities. He first came to Seattle in 1922 on an invitation to teach painting at the Cornish School (now the Cornish College of the Arts). Although Tobey only remained in this teaching position for a short period, he maintained deep ties to the Northwest for the rest of his career. His early work was primarily representational and was influenced by contemporary movements, such as Cubism, as well as a worldliness fed by his travels to England and Mexico (1931), Palestine (1932), China, France, Italy, and Japan (1934), and Canada (1935). After the 1930s, Tobey became increasingly preoccupied with the potential of line to convey energy and light. What came to be known as his "white writing" paintings were compositions characterized by interwoven calligraphic strokes that carried significant expressive power and usually covered the entire surface of the canvas. After a *LIFE* article titled "Mystic Painters of the Northwest," featuring Tobey, Guy Anderson, Kenneth Callahan, and Morris Graves, was published on September 28, 1953, all four artists gained increased national attention. Tobey was awarded a gold medal at the 1958 Venice Biennale and, in 1961, became the first American to exhibit paintings at the Louvre's Pavillon de Marsan. Represented in collections throughout the Pacific Northwest, Tobey's work is also owned by the Smithsonian American Art Museum, the Metropolitan Museum of Art, the Museum of Modern Art, and the Whitney Museum of American Art.

In 1962, Tobey's paintings were included in the Fountain Gallery's third show alongside the work of his fellow Washington-based artists Guy Anderson, Kenneth Callahan, Paul Horiuchi, and George Tsutakawa, highlighting Schnitzer's commitment to providing exposure to regional artists beyond Oregon. Tobey's *Two Market Figures* is an early work, the subjects of which are painted with a solidity to their forms that anchors them against the background. The wrinkled patterning from the paper, which Tobey embraced as a design element on the page, translates to a strong sense of unity throughout the composition, and the forms themselves appear to be radiating light or energy. Of this work, which hangs in her living room, Schnitzer said, "I'd always thought that that background, where he crinkled the paper, was kind of a forerunner of [his] white writing, because if you'll get up and look at that closely, and translate it in your mind, you'll see that it's like white writing."[1]

1 Interview with Schnitzer, September 15, 2011

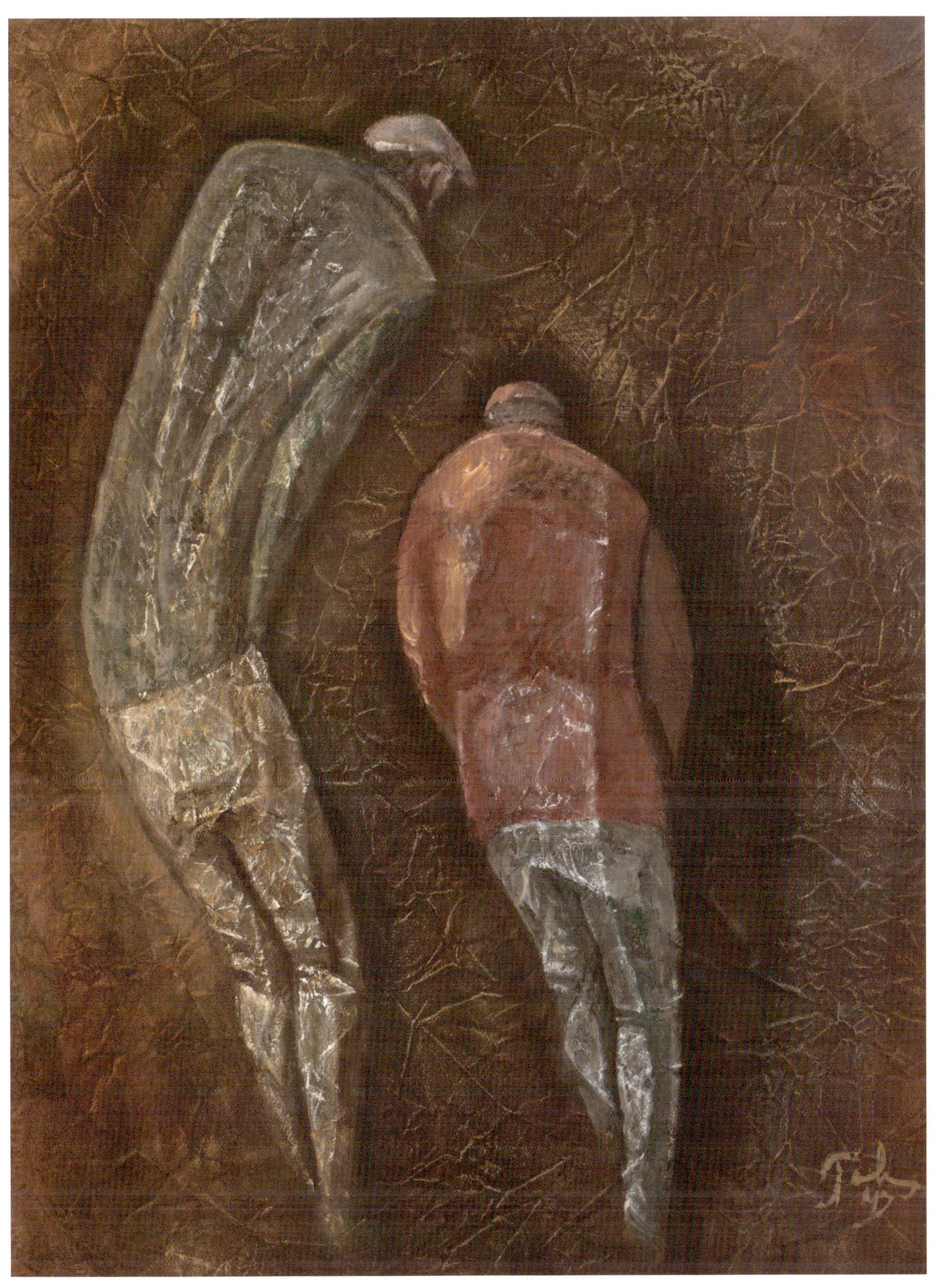

AFTERWORD

Organizing *Provenance* was both a challenge and a privilege. Our ambition is to honor Arlene Schnitzer for her commitments to artists and the growing creative community. The project allowed us into Schnitzer's life and gave us opportunities to learn from others who have known her longer and more intimately. We have selected and researched a mere fragment of the Arlene and Harold Schnitzer art collection. This pursuit is surely but one of more to follow that illustrates a storied life and contributions to our artistic heritage. *Provenance* also engaged Linda Tesner, director, Ronna and Eric Hoffman Gallery of Contemporary Art, Lewis & Clark College. Her essay reveals the impact of this unique collection and its distinctive founders on her personal understanding of art history. Mel Katz and Lucinda Parker, Portland artists, graciously shared their deep appreciation for Arlene Schnitzer and experiences at the Fountain Gallery. Biographies and provenances were researched and written by Danielle Knapp and our curatorial interns and art history graduate students Jeffrey Carlson, Jessica DiTillio, and Anne Taylor. Their contributions are core to our mission as a teaching institution, and they benefited immensely by investigating such rich and variegated resources as the collection of Arlene and Harold Schnitzer. We also thank the many art galleries that responded to our inquiries, especially Charles Froelick, at the Froelick Gallery, Portland; Greg Kucera, at the Kucera Gallery, Seattle; and Martha Lee and Katrina Woltze, at the Laura Russo Gallery, Portland. One very special collaborator was Laurie LaBathe. She works closely with Arlene Schnitzer, curating and managing an extensive collection of art, and has been involved in every detail of the project. This exhibition would not have come to fruition without her enthusiastic support and encouragement.

LAWRENCE FONG
Curator of American and Regional Art
Jordan Schnitzer Museum of Art

DANIELLE KNAPP
David McCosh Fellow Curator
Jordan Schnitzer Museum of Art

PERMISSIONS

ACE: Courtesy of the artist and Froelick Gallery, Portland, OR

ARNESON: Art © Estate of Robert Arneson/Licensed by VAGA, New York, NY

BACKSTRAND: Courtesy of the artist and the Laura Russo Gallery, Portland, OR

BARTOW: Courtesy of the artist and Froelick Gallery, Portland, OR

BUNCE: Courtesy of the Laura Russo Gallery, Portland, OR, for the Estate of Louis Bunce

COLESCOTT: Courtesy of the Laura Russo Gallery, Portland, OR, for the Estate of Robert Colescott

DE FOREST: Art © Estate of Roy De Forest/Licensed by VAGA, New York, NY

FEVES: Courtesy of Alan Feves

GRAVES: Courtesy of the Morris Graves Foundation, Loleta, CA

GRENON: Courtesy of the artist and the Laura Russo Gallery, Portland, OR

HORIUCHI: Courtesy of Paul M. Horiuchi and Vincent Horiuchi

JONES: Courtesy of the artist and the Laura Russo Gallery, Portland, OR

KANEKO: Courtesy of the artist and the Jun Kaneko Studio, Omaha, NE

KATZ: Courtesy of the artist and the Laura Russo Gallery, Portland, OR

LIBENSKÝ/BRYCHTOVÁ: Courtesy of the Heller Gallery, New York, NY

MARKOVITZ: Courtesy of the artist and the Greg Kucera Gallery, Seattle, WA

MORRIS, CARL: Courtesy of the Laura Russo Gallery, Portland, OR, for the Estate of Carl Morris

MORRIS, WILLIAM: Courtesy of the William Morris Studio, Stanwood, WA

OROPALLO: Courtesy of the artist and the Greg Kucera Gallery, Seattle, WA

PANDER: Courtesy of the artist and the Laura Russo Gallery, Portland, OR

PARKER: Courtesy of the artist and the Laura Russo Gallery, Portland, OR

PORTLAND: Courtesy of the artist and the Laura Russo Gallery, Portland, OR

RICKABAUGH: Courtesy of the artist and the Laura Russo Gallery, Portland, OR

RUSSO: Courtesy of the Laura Russo Gallery, Portland, OR, for the Estate of Michele Russo

TAKAMORI: Courtesy of the artist and the James Harris Gallery, Seattle, WA

TOBEY: © 2012 Estate of Mark Tobey / Artists Rights Society (ARS), New York, NY

This publication is made possible with generous support from Arlene Schnitzer/The Harold & Arlene Schnitzer CARE Foundation.

Issued in conjunction with the exhibition of the same title held May 12–September 16, 2012, Jordan Schnitzer Museum of Art, Eugene, Oregon.

LIBRARY OF CONGRESS CATALOGING-IN-PUBLICATION DATA

Provenance: In honor of Arlene Schnitzer, May 12–September 16, 2012 / Lawrence Fong, Danielle Knapp, and Linda Tesner. Pages cm. Issued in conjunction with the exhibition of the same title held May 12–September 16, 2012, Jordan Schnitzer Museum of Art, Eugene, Oregon. Curated by Lawrence Fong. Includes bibliographical references.

ISBN 978–0–87114–299–3

1. Art, American—Northwest, Pacific—20th century—Exhibitions. 2. Schnitzer, Arlene, 1929—Art collections—Exhibitions. 3. Art—Private collections—Oregon—Portland—Exhibitions. I. Schnitzer, Arlene, 1929-honouree. II. Fong, Lawrence M., curator. III. Jordan Schnitzer Museum of Art, host institution.
N6526.P76 2012 709.795'07479531—dc23 2012011913

Published by
JORDAN SCHNITZER MUSEUM OF ART
1430 Johnson Lane
1223 University of Oregon
Eugene, Oregon 97403–1223
541.346.3027
jsma.uoregon.edu

Lawrence Fong and Danielle Knapp, Editors
Diane Nelson, Designer
Photography by Richard Gehrke
Printed by Millcross Litho Incorporated, Portland, Oregon